WORDS
ON LOAN

WORLD ON LOAN

JOHN DAVIES

BIBLE SOCIETY

British and Foreign Bible Society
Stonehill Green, Westlea, SWINDON SN5 7DG, England

© John D. Davies 1993

First published 1993

All rights reserved. No part of this publication may be reproduced, stored in a retrieval system, or transmitted, in any form or by any means, electronic, mechanical, photocopying, recording or otherwise without the prior permission of The British and Foreign Bible Society. The right of John D. Davies to be identified as the author of this work has been asserted by him in accordance with the Copyright, Designs and Patents Act 1988.

Unless otherwise stated, quotations from the Bible are from the Good News Bible, published by the Bible Societies/HarperCollins © American Bible Society, New York. 1966, 1971 and 4th edition 1976.

A catalogue record for this book is available from the British Library

ISBN 0564 084654

Printed in Great Britain by Biddles Ltd, Guildford
Cover design by Jane Taylor

CONTENTS

FOREWORD

Many times in the history of the Church, renewal has come from small groups studying the Bible together. They discover that the Bible speaks to them and they see things in a new way. But it has also happened that the scholars have got hold of the Bible and locked it up, so that ordinary people think they cannot really understand it without the help of experts.

Bishop John Davies is a scholar who also has the gift of making the Bible come alive for ordinary people, so that they hear what God is saying. I am quite sure that those who use these studies will find that happening. It might be dangerous – it will certainly not be dull.

Lesslie Newbigin
Lent 1993

PREFACE

Several of the units in this book are adapted and enlarged from studies which appeared first in two courses which I produced for publication by The United Society for the Propagation of the Gospel: *Christ our Life,* published in cooperation with the Wrexham Council of Churches, the Diocese of Coventry, and the Diocese of St Asaph, 1982; and *Things of God,* published in cooperation with the Diocese of St Asaph, 1983. I am very grateful to USPG for agreeing to this use of the material.

A more detailed explanation of the method of this kind of Bible study can be found in *Mark at Work* by John D. Davies and John J. Vincent (Bible Reading Fellowship, 1986).

My concern about land–tenure and other central themes of Old Testament justice was first awakened by the demands of black Christians in South Africa, and developed by the small but vigorous book *My Neighbour's Landmark* by Frederick Verinder (Land and Liberty Press, 1911). These themes are well–developed in *Justice on the Agenda* by Roger Sainsbury (Marshalls, 1985), *Living as the People of God* by Christopher J. H. Wright (IVP, 1983), and in the various publications of the Land and Liberty Press, particularly *The Land and Biblical Economics* by Archer Torrey (1979). Many of these authors depend, very properly, on the vital but neglected work of Henry George, especially *Progress and Poverty* (first published in 1880). This is receiving new and critical application to modern social and ethical conditions in *From Wasteland to Promised Land* by Andelson and Dawsey (Shepheard–Walwyn, 1992).

I owe much to the writings of Jim Wallis, notably *The Call to Conversion* (Lion, 1981) and *Agenda for Biblical People* (Triangle, 1986), and to the writings of colleagues in the Jubilee Group, particularly Ken Leech's *The Social God.*

The background to Units 10–12 owes much to W. J. Hollenweger's "Intercultural Theology" in *Christian* Vol.6 No.1 (1980).

On the rarely tackled subject of the theology and ethics of taxation, there is much value in Bishop Stanley Booth–Clibborn's *Taxes, Burden or Blessing?* (Arthur James, 1991), and Tony Walter's *Fair Shares?* (Handsel Press, 1985).

The version of Psalm 24 with antiphon and music was composed by John Bell of the Iona Community (Wild Goose Publications).

On the specific subject of Christian Stewardship, there is a steady flow of helpful material from Church publishers, such as *Receiving and Giving* (Church House Publishing, 1990), and *Buried Treasure* (Methodist Publishing House, 1990). As a practical exercise in group study, there is much value in *Servants of Christ and Stewards of the Mysteries of God* prepared by Bishop B. N. Y. Vaughan when he was Bishop of Swansea and Brecon.

However, my main acknowledgement must be to the hundreds of people who have joined in Bible study groups on the lines of these studies over many years at Selly Oak, the Urban Theology Unit, Iona, in the Dioceses of St Asaph and Lichfield, and many other places. We learn best what the Bible has to teach us by putting ourselves under the authority of our sisters and brothers in the disciple–fellowship and discovering together where it takes us. No one who leads a Bible study like this should try to know all the answers in advance. Every sentence in these studies is really a quotation from someone or other: the only purpose of the design is to enable people's insights to flow. If this does not happen, if you find that the design is obstructing instead of enabling your work, break free from it; do not treat it as a rigid programme. Many of these studies have been developed from occasions when my wife, Shirley, and I have done a double–act. More than any other person, she is the source of the approach and the ideas of this book. What is more, she has been responsible for getting the whole text typed and prepared for the publishers — and that is a task of stewardship in itself.

SECTION A

INTRODUCTION

This is God's world.

That is the theme of this set of studies. We are in God's world: God's world is our past, present and future.

Almost every unit of this course has three phases:
- Getting Started
- Digging Deeper
- Practical Planning

(The one exception is a unit which really continues straight on from the previous one.)

The "Getting Started" part gets us to think about the world which we know. It starts where we are, with our own unique experience. At this point, we are all experts. Too often, study groups divide into talkative experts and silent "passengers": the "Getting Started" phase is designed to get everyone on board, to start with questions on which everyone is in some way an expert.

In the "Digging Deeper" phase we get into the Bible text. Here, quite properly, some people will know more than others. The person with expert knowledge can be valuable, but since most of the Bible passages are stories of one sort or another, their effectiveness depends not so much on knowledge as on how far we let our own imagination be taken into action by the story. That is, how much we let ourselves identify with what is going on in the story. The Jewish community has always been guided by the old stories of God's deliverance and God's law. Jesus told stories to get people to work things out for themselves; he stimulated their own wisdom — he did not strive to make them dependent upon his wisdom. So, in most of these units you will be asked to take part in the stories; to read them from the point of view of one character or another. Here you do need knowledge of the background, but you also need your own imagination.

The final phase is called "Practical Planning". This is the purpose of the whole exercise. You must leave sufficient time for it. If you have a total of, say, an hour and a half for your meeting, you should make sure that you move into this phase forty minutes before knocking–off time. You may easily be tempted to spend more time on delving into the past, into the endlessly fascinating details of the text: but if you miss out on the "Practical Planning" you will miss the fundamental purpose of your meeting. A meeting for Bible study is not primarily designed to give the members intellectual information or even spiritual riches. The purpose of such meetings is to provide an opportunity to change and develop the group, so that they can help to change and develop the Church, so that the Church can help to change and develop the world into being more truly God's Kingdom under God's authority. So the question is always, "what is the meaning of this portion of the Bible for us now?" If this is what God in action was like then, how is the same God wanting to act in our world now, through the Church, the body of Christ?

In some of these units, especially some of those dealing with the Old Testament, there are no particular "stage directions" in the "Digging Deeper" phase. This is because there is nothing wrong with ordinary straightforward discussion, and this may well be the best way of handling this sort of material. Some members of the group may think that the law of God is very attractive; others that it is all very well but not practicable; others that it is plain contrary to human nature. Fine, doubtless there were these various opinions, and others, to be heard among the people who originally received and treasured these laws. We still have to work out how to put these values into action in our own day.

But most of the units invite the group to break up into small teams, to look at a situation from different angles. Do not worry if these teams are very small — a group of six people can work in three teams of two. The secret is to feel your way into the story and imagine what it is like to be there. You will find that some are easier than others. Many of the Bible readings are from *The Dramatised Bible,* which is a wonderful encouragement to us to get into the stories of the Bible imaginatively. But don't let this discourage people from bringing their own Bibles. It is often valuable to compare different translations or versions. Printed extracts, to some extent, will always misrepresent the text, because they pull the extract out from its place in the whole story.

When you divide into teams, do everything you can to get each team to feel its identity — stick a label on the wall beside each team, saying "Jesus", "Paul", "Jerusalem", or whatever. Or, better still, give people sticky labels to wear. When the teamwork is over, make sure that the labels are removed and people start to be "themselves" again.

Too often, Bible study courses are designed as if the Church consisted only of adults. But the school of God is for adults, young people, and children together. Sometimes, on a journey, children will see things before the adults do — they run ahead and get a different view. At other times, they follow, or are carried. There are some units of this course (such as 2, 3, 4, 7, 8, 9, 13, 14) which could quite easily be handled by groups of children and young people. A church could have separate groups for different ages, following more or less the same programme of themes and exchanging findings from time to time. Or, for some of the units, you could arrange all-age Bible studies and adapt the designs as necessary. Some young people move quickly and imaginatively into roles and can lead adults into seeing what is going on in the stories. This is especially important with the subject-matter of this book. Young people are sometimes more alert than most adults to questions of the stewardship of creation: and it is never too early for young people to recognize their responsibility for stewardship within the Church, to be givers as well as receivers.

So, as an ice-breaker, here is a kind of mini-unit, with elements which could work with people of all ages.

GETTING STARTED

Invite people to bring with them to the meeting some "proper" plants — flowers or vegetables — and also some weeds. Let everyone describe their plants and weeds to the rest of the group. Who says that a weed is a weed? Why?

DIGGING DEEPER

JESUS' PARABLE OF THE WEEDS
Matthew 13.24–30

Jesus   *The Kingdom of heaven is like this. A man sowed good seed in his field. One night, when everyone was asleep, an enemy came and sowed weeds among the wheat and went away. When the plants grew and the ears of corn began to form, then the weeds showed up. The man's servants came to him and said:*

Servant	*Sir, it was good seed you sowed in your field; where did the weeds come from?*
Jesus	*He answered:*
Man	*It was some enemy who did this.*
Servant	*Do you want us to go and pull up the weeds?*
Man	*No, because as you gather the weeds you might pull up some of the wheat along with them. Let the wheat and the weeds both grow together until harvest. Then I will tell the harvest workers to pull up the weeds first, tie them in bundles and burn them, and then to gather in the wheat and put it in my barn.*

Divide the group up into three teams, a wheat team, a weed team, and a farmer team. Each member of the wheat team and the weed team makes a label saying "wheat" or "weed" as the case may be.

Questions for the wheat and weed teams separately:

- What are we good for?

- What are our rights?

- Why should we be allowed to survive?

Questions for the farmer team:

- What am I to do if the wheat and the weeds get mixed up?

- What are the options and policies open to me?

- What are the alternatives?

- What are the snags?

After a few minutes, the wheat and weed teams come together and mingle, standing closely to each other on the floor.

Questions for the farmer:

• What are you going to do about the weeds?

In normal circumstances the farmer's answer would be:

"Get the weeds out."

• Why?

"Because they take the space and they take the nourishment which I want the wheat to have."

All right — we pull the weeds out — the members of the weed team move away from the wheat.

But will this work in every case? The members of the weed team move back to where they were mingled with the wheat, and they each wrap their ankles round the ankles of the wheat team.

Again the farmer faces the question:

• What are you going to do about these weeds?

Let the farmer team decide!

The point of Jesus' story is that the particular weed he was talking about was darnel — a weed which, in the early stages of its growth, looks very like wheat. Darnel produces a seed which people would call useless because it is poisonous to humans; but, in fact, it is quite good for fuel.

PRACTICAL PLANNING

This parable is a stewardship story.

• Why is our church (or our Sunday school, or our study group) allowed to survive?

Perhaps we are allowed to survive because we really are growing for God. We are productive. We are nourishing the world around.

Or, perhaps we are allowed to survive because God feels that to pull us up would cause more problems than it would solve.

The mere fact that our church or Sunday school or study group exists is not necessarily a sign that God is happy with it. We may, perhaps, be absorbing energy ourselves and not growing anything for the benefit of anyone else. Are we a "weed–church" or a "wheat–church"? Probably we are a mixture. But a stewardship programme will fail if it is only a scheme to enable us to survive — God may tolerate weeds but he won't put fertilizer on them!

Look at what your church does, week by week, and make a list of the ways in which it is truly growing for the sake of the world around: notice the ways in which God is working through you. This will put you in touch with the basic stewardship question.

• What does God want us for?

If you make this kind of note at the end of your "Practical Planning", this can start you on making a kind of cumulative workbook which will build up over your series of meetings. At the end, you will be able to look back and see what practical action the Holy Spirit has been suggesting to you. The questions should include:

• What should I be doing?

• What should our group be doing?

• What should we be encouraging others to do?

SECTION A

UNIT 1　STEWARDSHIP — MANAGEMENT FOR GOD

GETTING STARTED

A steward is a manager. The manager's task is to serve the interests of the owner. Christian stewardship is the management of all our resources on behalf of God.

A typical Christian gathering is a gathering of managers to consult with God. The consultation will include sharing our experience of success and failure; it will include concern about staff: it will include reflection on policy: it will include sharing of resources. Above all, it will be a gathering of people who are trying to make sure that their ideas and programme fit and fulfil the purposes for which the company exists, the objectives for which the movement was founded. So we have the basic idea of any meeting of Christians, whether it be a finance committee, a Eucharist, or a prayer meeting. There will be some study of the Bible, some prayer for each other and the world, some acknowledgement of failure and achievement in confession and thanksgiving. And, above all, there will be worship. When we worship, as Christians, we bend our minds and imaginations and motives to fit God's mind and God's intentions. The wavelength and wave–pattern of our human spirit are adjusted to coincide with the Holy Spirit. Our value–system is corrected by God's values. This is what true worship is about. Its effectiveness is not to be measured by whether it gives us a high — the Holy Spirit is not in business just to provide people with a steady supply of spiritual experiences. True worship happens when people meet God and are put effectively in touch with his programme and his purposes. Worship is the point of contact between God and his managers.

You may feel, at the start, that this idea of "management" means that stewardship is not for you. "Me, part of the management? Never!" All right, it's not a perfect word or image. But why does it cause problems? The difficulty is that, in our society, "managers" are a small number of people at the top who exercise responsibility, and they organize lots of other people who don't have responsibility. But that is a misleading picture. A woman with little money, not much formal education, and three children to look after on her own will have to be as shrewd and competent in managing as any tycoon. And one of the messages which comes over most strongly from the Bible, in both Old and New Testaments, is that we all have responsibility, we all have contributions to make. If there is not a management–contribution from the weak towards the strong, from the poor towards the rich, from the child towards the adult, something is badly missing. And the chances are that we won't get it right just by studying, because that usually gives advantage to those who have had the educational advantage already. We are more likely to be corrected by the kind of worship which puts our values alongside God's values and renews our vision of God and of each other.

DIGGING DEEPER

So, let us start with an act of worship, using one of the oldest songs from our traditional song–book, the Psalms.

THE EARTH IS THE LORD'S
Psalm 24

> *ANTIPHON*   *The earth is the Lord's*
> *and all that is in it*
> *the world and its people*
> *belong to the Lord.*

> *Verse 1 Cantor A* *All that exists, all creatures and kinds,*
> *all women and men to their maker belong;*
> *under the seas God founded the earth*
> *and planted it firm in the depths of the*
> *waves.*

> *Verse 2 Cantor B* *Who may go up to the mountain of God*
> *and who may appear in the Lord's holy*
> *place?*
> *Cantor A* *The one with clean hands, whose heart is*
> *kept pure,*
> *who shuns what is false and forsakes all*
> *deceit.*

> *Verse 3 Cantor A* *Those who receive the blessing of God*
> *know that their salvation is found in the*
> *Lord.*

> Cantor B This is the witness of those who enquire,
> who long for the presence of Jacob's own
> God.

> Verse 4 Chorus Fling wide the gates and open the doors
> and so let the great King of Glory come in.
> Cantor A Who is this king to enter these gates?
> Chorus The Lord strong and mighty in battle is he.

> Verse 5 Chorus Gates everlasting, now lift yourselves up
> that the great king of glory might enter
> within.
> Cantor A Who is this king that the gates should be
> raised?
> Chorus The mighty and strong Lord of hosts is his
> name.

This can be said or sung (the music is printed at the back of this book on page 100). The antiphon should be said or sung by everyone after each verse.

A Psalm such as this needs this sort of treatment because it is essentially a conversation, in which the different characters lead each other in their quest.

The *Antiphon* is the song of the whole people of God, making a statement about the whole creation. *Cantor A* represents the priestly establishment, those who are responsible for safeguarding faith and tradition, the citizens of the community of holiness. *Cantor B* and *Chorus* represent the pilgrim community, the enquirers, the searchers, the travellers, those who haven't got there yet.

The song starts with the responsible citizens stating the universal truths and standards of the creator. This is God's world. He made it according to his own design, to include all in his purpose of order and justice. The pilgrims ask their questions and are given the traditional answer, that what God requires is honesty and lack of fraud in people's dealing with each other. Access to God in worship requires proper stewardship in political, economic, and personal justice.

The pilgrims then turn the whole conversation around. Instead of merely seeking admission for themselves, they claim that the great king of glory is not safely inside the city with the priests and citizens but is with them outside, demanding access. The citizens have erected their structures to exclude others and keep themselves secure: God requires that these gates are raised so that he and his fellow–travellers can enter. The priests admit their ignorance:

"Who is this King?" The citizens tell them, in no uncertain terms.
The priests seem to say, "Sorry, we didn't quite catch that: would
you mind repeating it?" And the answer comes crashing across —
"The Lord of hosts, your Lord and ours."

We have a similar pattern when the Lord, God incarnate in
Jesus, comes to the holy city, Jerusalem. The pilgrims who have
travelled with him from Galilee, and the crowds (the landless peasant communities), sing their Hosannas. The secure citizens of the
capital, who have all the advantages of communication and access
to the Temple, have to ask, "Who is this?" The answer comes from
those from outside, those on the fringe: "This is Jesus, the prophet
from Nazareth of Galilee — we can tell you, he's come with us,
he's from the far north like we are." And Jesus proceeds to claim
his own access to the city and the Temple, and then to make access
for other people who get squeezed out by the conventions of religion, the Gentiles, the disabled, and the children (Matthew
21.8–16).

"The earth is the Lord's" is a claim that sounds very simple and
conventional. But it is a controversial claim which set Israel apart
from other nations, just as Jesus got into final trouble with the religious and civic leaders of his own day on account of his treatment
of the Temple. For the nations round about Israel, the earth was
not the property of a single God, but it was divided up into tribal
areas, each with its God, each with its sovereignty. This was, and
is, a thoroughly credible theology. Most of our experience tells us
that the land is divided through ownership, that wealth is split up
among groups and nations competing with each other, each having
its own sphere of interest, its own value–system, its own divinity.
Idolatry depends on this division of human interest. Your idol
stands for your group, mine stands for mine. Idolatry makes good
sense of the way things are, and so it was always seen by the spiritual leaders of the Bible as the most dangerous of all lies.

The earth is the Lord's. The land itself, which is the basic
source of all our production, belongs to God, long before it can be
called the property of individuals, nations, or corporations. The
wealth that results from human labour is the Lord's — not just the
money on the church collection plate, but the money in our bank
accounts, the money which is paid in taxes, the money used in the
world's debt–systems, the money which enables trade and
exchange.

The earth is the Lord's. This is not, like our "Private Property"
notices, a threat. It is not, primarily, a law or a doctrine. It is a

song, a celebration. Despite the waste of energy used in keeping up hostilities, despite the over–use of resources by groups of producers in competition with each other, despite the debt–system which traps so many, despite the many ways in which people are separated from the land and have no access to it or responsibility for it, the earth is still the Lord's. This is the song of those who defy the obvious experience of the world. It is the song of those who are willing to be stewards and managers of God's world.

PRACTICAL PLANNING

Could you use this version of Psalm 24 in worship? It would need to be sung or said by the whole congregation plus two groups, one stationary in the sanctuary area, one moving into the church as pilgrims.

Many psalms have found their way into Christian hymn books in some form. Do you know of a version of Psalm 24, or a hymn which expresses the same ideas? If not, it would seem that this wonderful song has been strangely neglected in Christian worship. Why do you think this is?

The bread, wine, and money are placed on the table in our churches, and represent all the earth, all things, all that is both natural and manufactured, and all wealth generated. Can you think of ways in which, occasionally, this aspect of our worship could be made more significant?

UNIT 2 THIS IS GOD'S WORLD

GETTING STARTED

Get into small teams and look back on your last harvest festival.
You could use these questions to help you reflect.

- Who remembers what?

- What did you do personally?

- How did you contribute?

Of the total group:

- How many brought an offering of their own to the festival?

- How many worked on the festival?

- How many remember anything specific about the sermon?

- What word or phrase would you use to describe your harvest festival?

Beautiful	Productive
Traditional	Happy
New	Friendly
Expensive	Impressive
Profitable	The same old thing

- Can you think of other words to describe it?

DIGGING DEEPER

The following passage can be read aloud by two people, one reading the narrative and one the declaration of the worshipper.

Deuteronomy 26. 1–12

When you come into the land, which the Lord your God is giving you to occupy as your patrimony, and settle in it, you shall take the first fruits of all the produce of the soil, which you gather in from the land which the Lord your God is giving, and put them in a basket. Then you shall go to the place which the Lord your God will choose as a dwelling for his name and come to the priest, whoever he shall be in those days. You shall say to him "I declare this day to the Lord your God that I have entered the land which the Lord swore to our forefathers to give us." The priest shall take the basket from your hand and set it down before the altar of the Lord your God. Then you shall solemnly recite before the Lord your God: "My father was a homeless Aramean who went down to Egypt with a small company and lived there until they became a great, powerful and numerous nation. But the Egyptians ill–treated us, humiliated us and imposed cruel slavery upon us. Then we cried to the Lord the God of our fathers for help, and he listened to us and saw our humiliation, our hardship and distress: and so the Lord brought us out of Egypt with a strong hand and outstretched arm, with terrifying deeds, and with signs and portents. He brought us to this place and gave us this land, a land flowing with milk and honey. And now I have brought the first fruits of the soil which thou, O Lord, has given me." You shall then set the basket before the Lord your God and bow down in worship before him. You shall all rejoice, you and the Levites and the aliens living among you, for all the good things which the Lord your God has given to you and to your family.

When you have finished taking a tithe of your produce in the third year, you shall give it to the Levites and to the aliens, the orphans and the widows. They shall eat it in your settlements and be well fed.

Now divide into two teams (A and B) to examine the process described in the passage using the following questions.

Team A: In what ways is this process similar to our harvest festival?

Team B: In what ways is this process different from our harvest festival?

When the teams come together, they tell each other their findings. The leader should note the lists of similarities and differences. Which team has the longest list?

You need to notice at least the following points about the Deuteronomy passage.

1. The process that this passage describes is part of the law of God. The whole of this law is very much concerned with land, wealth, production, and distribution.

2. It is about recognizing God as the owner and ruler of the physical world, the world of wealth, power, economics etc. Before people claim any product for their own profit or for their own use, they are required to bring the first fruits of their work to God, acknowledging him as the owner and giver of all.

3. The passage describes how the person bringing the offering is required to recite the story of God's creation of us, his people, out of slavery. Once we were all powerless people, with no rights, no land, and no power over the product of our labour. Now we have something of our own to offer, but it isn't really our own — it belongs to God and is to be shared with those who don't have land and cannot support themselves: the Levite, the stranger, the widow etc. (Levites were a tribe who served the temple and had no land, and therefore could grow no crops of their own.) We are not making our offering simply because we are glad to have a harvest, but because God has given us a place in his programme of making justice and creating wealth to be shared. God is worthy of our obedience and our worship, not just because he favours us but because his whole design makes sense and we gladly share in it. Year by year, we are reminded of his good purpose and of his dependability as the one who gives us land and the power to work with him in his plan.

4. What is offered is not the best or most beautiful produce: it is simply the first harvest to ripen, the first product to be ready for use. It is not a display but a payment of what is due to God as the owner. It is a first instalment of our duty to use all the products of land and labour according to God's will — a kind of tax. Nowadays we tend to regard all

our income as our own, and to resent taxation as the government interfering and depriving us of what belongs properly to us. But, according to this text, none of our wealth is strictly our own, God has first claim upon it. So this tax is part of our obedience to God, and it is a form of celebration and worship.

5. The offering of the first fruits has no fixed proportion; it is part of the law of God which "rises to the majestic heights of the unenforceable" (Martin Luther King).

6. In addition to the first fruits, there is a requirement for a more definite percentage of income, the tithe. This is specifically to provide for the most disadvantaged members of society and, indeed, for immigrants and other outsiders. These people are to share the well–being of the settled communities. The law of God requires that there should be no people left poor and unsupported. This law is too important to be left to the unreliable motive of private generosity. It is a principle which has to be reflected in the public accountability, part of the corporate will of the whole community. Without this, there can be no reliable budgeting, and the poor are left to depend on the whims and emotions of the rich. Even our ability to create wealth is limited by this principle — the farmer is not to extract all possible produce from fields, vineyards, and fruit trees, but is to leave some to be gathered by those who have no land rights (Leviticus 19.9–10; Deuteronomy 24.19–22). (It is worth noting that, by the time of Jesus, taxation had taken on a much less satisfactory form. Tax collectors were hated because it was their job to extract as much money as possible from the people of the land to maintain a foreign army of occupation and an oppressive colonial system. In this form, taxation was not a sign of justice but a sign of a new slavery. There was no provision of revenue for social welfare, the sharing of wealth with the poor, which is the characteristic element of God's justice.)

Our harvest festivals usually come at the end of the harvest period — "all is safely gathered in". The exact purpose of this ceremony in Deuteronomy corresponds better to our Christian tradition of Lammas Day (1 August) when we offer the loaf from flour milled from the year's first crop of wheat. A lot of the meaning of this passage could nevertheless be expressed in our harvest festivals.

But how far does this happen?

PRACTICAL PLANNING

How could we express these truths better? What differences in our
worship would make sense?

Consider these points for discussion:

1. How could we develop the harvest festival, so that it is not
   only a display of our achievement but also an offering of
   the value of our work?

   (If our products were offered in this way, it would be right
   and proper to sell them for church funds — as is common
   in other parts of the world. Do you agree?)

2. The harvest festival seems increasingly to be a display of
   pretty things rather than an offering of our ability to create
   wealth.

   How can it be made more representative of a wider range
   of human work?

   How can this be done so as to honour the contribution of
   the unemployed, the disabled, the pensioners, and not to
   exclude them?

3. Could we strengthen the tradition of the offering of the
   first fruits on Lammas Day?

   Could we develop a custom of making a public contribution at the offertory at the Communion when we start
   something new — the first product from a new sewing
   machine, the first bit of writing we get published, the first
   hour's wage from a new job, the profit from the year's first
   bit of trading etc.?

4. Much of God's work of caring, educating, and other services is done now by government, paid for by compulsory
   rates and taxes.

   Can you think of any way in which this compulsory payment could also be made a spiritual offering, a willing obedience to God?

What consequences are there if you come to the conclusion that some of the purposes for which your taxes are taken are contrary to the will of God?

5. Finally, a typical stewardship question to take home and think about and, perhaps, to act on:

Which do you think is closer to the mind of God, to give time and money for charitable causes, or to work for improved conditions for the poor through higher taxation?

UNIT 3   STEWARDS OF THE WORLD

GETTING STARTED

Take a few minutes to think about the following questions.

- What are you in charge of?

- What have you been in charge of in the past?

- Can you remember the first time you took charge of something?

- Make a list of things you have been in charge of.

- What do you feel about being in charge — pride, anxiety, responsibility — what?

DIGGING DEEPER

GENESIS 1.26—2.4
(From *The Dramatised Bible*)

Narrator   *...Then God said:*

God   *And now we will make human beings; they will be like us and resemble us. They will have power over the fish, the birds, and all animals, domestic and wild, large and small.*

Narrator   *So God created human beings, making them to be like himself. He created them male and female, blessed them, and said:*

God   *Have many children, so that your descendants will live all over the earth and bring it under their control. I am putting you in charge of the fish, the birds, and all the wild animals. I have provided all kinds of grain and all kinds of fruit for you to eat; but for all the wild animals and for all the birds I have provided grass and leafy plants for food.*

> *Narrator*   *And it was done. God looked at everything he had made, and he was very pleased. Evening passed and morning came — that was the sixth day. And so the whole universe was completed. By the seventh day God finished what he had been doing and stopped working. He blessed the seventh day and set it apart as a special day, because by that day he had completed his creation and stopped working. And that is how the universe was created.*

In this extract from *The Dramatised Bible* God says to the human beings, "I am putting you in charge of the fish, the birds, and all the wild animals." Traditional translations of this passage use the word "dominion" or "rule". This has encouraged people to feel that they can do what they like with the rest of God's creation — exploit it, use it as a plaything, fight over it. If God puts us "in charge" of the rest of creation it means that he is commissioning us to manage it for him, to take responsibility for it, to be his stewards. This means, certainly, that humans have some authority over the rest of creation: but it also means that the rest of creation has a claim upon human beings. It is a two–way relationship.

This is all part of the covenant theme which runs right through the Bible. God makes a covenant between himself and human beings, and between himself and the rest of creation. In each direction, there are rights and responsibilities. Human beings are answerable to God for their stewardship of the rest of creation. God speaks to us through our grandchildren, who ask us, "What kind of condition is the earth going to be in when we grow up? Please leave this earth in the condition in which you would like to find it."

The text does particularly stress living creatures, animals, fish and birds. They most obviously register the effects of human cruelty and carelessness, in pollution and mass–destruction. To take this seriously is proper stewardship, not mere childish sentimentality.

The task of being in charge of creation is given to humankind as a whole. Access to the resources of Earth is open to all the human race, not just to those who succeed in grabbing the levers of power. A great deal of the waste and pollution of the earth happens not because of ignorance or carelessness, but because people use things in their fighting against other people. War permits destruction which would never be tolerated for any other purpose. Companies and nations in competition with each other use raw materials to make more products than are strictly necessary. So, as a human race, we can no longer say that the earth is our earth. Because we have become strangers to each other, we have become strangers to the earth.

We buy land, and say, "This is mine and not yours." So we accumulate "dominion" for ourselves over and against each other. We get security for ourselves and, whether we intend this or not, we get our security at the expense of someone else's. Those who can afford to do so connive in pushing up the price of land; and homelessness increases.

Being a steward is a task. It involves work. Management is a responsible job. Work is part of God's command and covenant. It is, of course, something much greater than paid employment. The conceiving and bearing and nurturing of children, according to this passage from Genesis, is a primary work for God. In our present way of life, the production of things seems to be reckoned as much more economically important than the production of people. Care for children starts to be taken seriously, in political and economic terms, only when they start to be of school age, when their basic shaping has already been done, when their most fundamental education is over.

Again, the mandate to work is given to the whole human race. To prevent another person from working, to tolerate conditions which prevent another person from taking part in the stewarding task, is a fault in our own stewarding. Unemployment may have many causes, but, above all, it starts when people have no access to the land and no way of taking responsibility for the land. In fact, unemployment is a sign that our stewardship of creation has gone wrong. Our value–systems have failed. Our worship is incomplete.

Work is important. But it is not the most important thing about people. The most important thing is not what you are but who you are. Who you are is a person, made in the image and likeness of God, a sister or brother of Jesus Christ. It is this relationship which comes first. We trust in the relationship — it is our security. It puts us in one status with all other children of God: we are born and baptized as equally loved. We are nourished equally on the body and blood of Christ. Unless this really does come first, our stewarding may easily become a way of earning, status or reward. When that happens, our unity is broken. Those who have the opportunity to be successful will become successful, and others will be labelled as failures. We will be valued — and we may even value ourselves — in terms of our productive ability and not simply because we are fellow–children of God. When that happens, we find ourselves to be slaves, rivals to each other. A church which is keen on stewardship has to watch carefully to see that it does not drift into a two–tier system of membership, the valuable members and the less valuable. As we shall see, the law of God always starts with what God has done for us. This is why stewardship is rightly called "Christian response" (see Galatians 4.7; John 15.15; Hebrews 3.5–6).

Who you are is a matter of your relationships, to God and other people. If it becomes too much a matter of nation or tribe, it can lead us into racism. What you are is a matter of your skills, training or achievement. If this becomes too important, if our occupation or our success becomes the overriding truth about us, it can become something which we might call "jobism". Just as racism makes second–class persons — or non–persons — out of those who are not of the favoured tribe, so jobism makes second–class persons, or non–persons, out of those who don't succeed in the search for work.

But one of the marvellous values of work is its extraordinary variety. Work is our task of turning things of nature into culture. It is making order through developing language and systems of symbols (Genesis 2.19–20). God's purpose is, evidently, to encourage the human species to develop in as great a variety as possible, preserving and affirming a wide range of languages, cultures, and ways of life (Genesis 11; Acts 2.5–12). One nation's tanks and missiles are likely to be difficult to distinguish from those of another; but their hymnbooks, liturgies, and buildings are likely to be very different. A good stewarding Church will be united in its worship and in community with other Churches: but within its fellowship there will be opportunity for every possibility of language and musical style, and every age group. The Church is not, and never has been, limited to one language and one culture. In Britain, there has never been just one Christian culture, and there certainly is not one now.

PRACTICAL PLANNING

> • Look around your own area. How far do you think people are being responsible in their handling of their environment?

Think of some examples of good practice and bad practice. How can you help to encourage good practice, in home, at school, at work, in shops etc.?

How "green" is your church? — in its use of recycled paper, its use of fuel etc.?

- Justice, peace, and care for creation all belong together. How can your church help in the formation of public opinion?

Should it become a pressure–group or watchdog?

- In your church, how much do you know about each other's work? How far do you share with each other the problems, puzzles, opportunities and satisfactions of your different experiences of work?

How far have you heard and shared the experiences of unemployed people?

If strangers come into your church, how far would they be able to get an idea of the work done in your area, by looking around your church building?

- To what extent does your church include all the languages (including musical languages) used by the members?

How far does it represent the variety of different types of people in your area?

- What are you going to do about any of these questions?

SECTION B
OLD TESTAMENT LAW

INTRODUCTION

The next three units explore further the meaning of "The Earth is the Lord's." To be a steward means to have responsibility, and to use power on behalf of the owner or the master. As the people of God, our stewardship is not limited to functions of the Church. Though it may surprise some of us to realize it, most of God's concerns do not come directly under the authority of Church Councils and Synods! In this section we look at three basic ways in which power works and in which stewardship is exercised.

The majority of main passages for study in these units are not well-known. So the "Digging Deeper" sections do not offer any particular process for handling them. People will probably find a good deal of interest just in reading the full text and checking the many cross-references which are supplied in, for example, the Revised Standard Version or the New Jerusalem Bible. Share with each other the points which you find new, interesting, or puzzling. Note how often someone will say, "I didn't know the Bible had anything to say about that!" Ask, from time to time, "Would that work today in this country? If not, why not?" Face up to the question, "Is this just irrelevant past history?" There are certainly some elements in Leviticus for instance, which Christians believe no longer apply, because of new values brought through Jesus. But that does not mean that we can choose to ignore the emphasis placed on justice as a priority in these passages.

UNIT 4 LAND

GETTING STARTED

- What is the place where you meet?

- You are (unless you are in a ship or aircraft) on a piece of land — often called a "property". Who owns it? Since when? How did this ownership happen?

- Are you a landowner? What area do you own? What is its value? What was its value when you first acquired it? (Note, we are thinking about the land itself, not about the structures which human beings have built on it.) If it has increased in value, why is this? Whose work has caused it to become more valuable — yours or someone else's? Who should get the benefit of this increase in value?

Some people find it difficult to realize just how different land is from any other property. We don't make it ourselves, nor does anyone else. There is a strictly limited amount of it. Most things, like cars or clothes, decline in value with age; land tends to increase in value, even when it is not improved or developed. The increase in value is often caused by the activities of the community as a whole, for instance the building of a motorway: but most of the profit goes to the landowner.

- Do you know of people who are unable to get a house? Is this because the price of housing has risen so much over the last fifteen years or so? Or because Local Authorities have got so few council houses for rent? Or are there other reasons?

DIGGING DEEPER

LEVITICUS 25.8–34 (extracts)

You are to count off seven sabbaths of years, that is seven times seven years, forty–nine years, and in the seventh month, on the tenth day of the month, on the Day of

Atonement, you are to send the ram's horn throughout your land to sound a blast. Hallow the fiftieth year and proclaim liberation in the land for all its inhabitants. It is to be a jubilee year for you: each of you is to return to his holding, everyone to his family.

In the year of jubilee every one of you is to return to his holding. When you sell or buy land amongst yourselves, neither party must exploit the other. You must pay your fellow–countryman according to the number of years since the jubilee, and he must sell to you according to the remaining number of annual crops. The more years there are to run, the higher the price; the fewer the years, the lower, because what he is selling you is a series of crops. You must not victimize one another, but fear your God, because I am the Lord your God.

No land may be sold outright, because the land is mine, and you come to it as aliens and tenants of mine. Throughout the whole land you hold, you must allow a right of redemption over land which has been sold.

When a man sells a dwelling–house in a walled town, he must retain the right of redemption till a full year has elapsed after the sale: for that time he has the right of redemption. If it is not redeemed before a full year is out, the house in the walled town will belong for ever to the buyer and his descendants; it does not revert to its former owner at the jubilee. But houses in unwalled hamlets are to be treated as property in the open country; the right of redemption will hold good, and in any case the house reverts at the jubilee.

Levites are to have the perpetual right to redeem houses which they hold in towns belonging to them. If one of the Levites does not redeem his house in such a town, then it will still revert to him at the jubilee, because the houses in Levite towns are their holding in Israel. The common land surrounding their towns cannot be sold, because it is their property in perpetuity.

Anyone who thinks that the Bible isn't about economic and political affairs should have a look at Leviticus 25! This adds a bit more substance to the belief that "The Earth is the Lord's".

1. The land belongs to God, and people — even the king — are his tenants. They look after and manage the land for God. People are stewards for God, in charge of the land, responsible for its maintenance and just sharing.

2. Consequently, no individual person can claim permanent and outright (or, as we would say, freehold) possession of land. Land changes hands for all sorts of reasons — commercial success, hard work, or luck. But the law here says that these changes of ownership are for a limited period only: at the fiftieth year, the land reverts to its original owner. So every family keeps a stake in the land, and the value of the land is kept down. All that can be sold is the right to use the land for a specific length of time. It is the kind of land–tenure system which many traditional people in various parts of the world have had: they would no more think of selling land than we would think of selling air. The deepest anger among black South Africans is because they thought that they were selling the right to use the land to white people, and white people thought that they were buying land freehold. Deep down, this sense of being cheated out of their ancestral land is the strongest motive in their struggle.

3. The jubilee law was designed to prevent the people of Israel splitting into a small number of landowners on the one hand, and a large number of landless, dispossessed, debt–trapped paupers on the other. The idea was not that everyone should have exactly the same — which would be impossible with the wide variety of types of land in Palestine — but that every family should have enough to be able to claim a stake in the land, and to share in responsibility for the land.

4. Levites were a special case. As a tribe, they did not have an allocation of land, because their task in temple services required them to live in the town. In the town, outright buying and selling of properties in perpetuity was allowed. Because they had no land, they received a regular income, in cash or in kind, from the rest of the people. This was not a clergy salary: it was compensation, compensation paid by those who had possession of land to those who had no possession of land (Numbers 18.21–29).

> 5. All this is the law of God for the people whom he has set
> free from slavery. This refrain comes in almost every para-
> graph: "I am the LORD your God who brought you out of
> slavery to give you this land." This, therefore, is what it
> means to be a liberated people, a redeemed community.
> Remember what you were, and what has happened to you.
> Be true to the deliverance and salvation which you have
> received (see Exodus 20.2 — the most important part of
> the Ten Commandments). This is what the Sabbath is all
> about. Therefore, a just economic sharing is totally bound
> up with true worship.

We can see the same teaching being needed hundreds of years later
— about 500 years before Christ. The Jewish people had been
taken off into a new slavery, in exile in Babylon. Later, some of
them were able to come back and set themselves up again in the
land. Their leader, Nehemiah, saw that the people had forgotten
the old laws; a few were grabbing the land, and the others were
getting into debt. So he intervened to restore God's justice. Later,
he wrote an account of this episode. As storyteller, he gives his
story of what he said as Governor.

NEHEMIAH 5.1–13
(From *The Dramatised Bible*)

Old Nehemiah	*Many of the people, both men and women, began to complain against their fellow–Jews [some said]:*
Woman 1	*We have large families, we need corn to keep us alive.*
[Old Nehemiah	*Others said:]*
Man 1	*We have had to mortgage our fields and vineyards and houses to get enough corn to keep us from starving.*
[Old Nehemiah	*Still others said:]*
Man 2	*We had to borrow money to pay the royal tax on our fields and vineyards.*

Woman 2	*We are of the same race as our fellow Jews. Aren't our children just as good as theirs? But we have to make slaves of our children.*
Man 1	*Some of our daughters have already been sold as slaves.*
Woman 1	*We are helpless because our fields and vineyards have been taken away from us.*
Old Nehemiah	*When I heard their complaints, I was angry and decided to act. I denounced the leaders and officials of the people and told them:*
Young Nehemiah	*You are oppressing your brothers!*
Old Nehemiah	*I called a public assembly to deal with the problem and said:*
Young Nehemiah	*As far as we have been able, we have been buying back our Jewish brothers who had to sell themselves to foreigners. Now you are forcing your own brothers to sell themselves to you, their fellow-Jews!*
Old Nehemiah	*The leaders were silent and could find nothing to say. Then I said:*
Young Nehemiah	*What you are doing is wrong! You ought to obey God and do what's right. Then you would not give our enemies, the Gentiles, any reason to ridicule us. I have let the people borrow money and corn from me. Now let's give up all our claims to repayment. Cancel all the debts they owe you — money or corn or wine or olive oil. And give them back their fields, vineyards, olive groves, and houses at once!*

Old Nehemiah	*The leaders replied:*
Leader 1	*We'll do as you say.*
Leader 2	*We'll give the property back and not try to collect the debts.*
Old Nehemiah	*I called in the priests and made the leaders swear in front of them to keep the promise they had just made. Then I took off the sash I was wearing round my waist and shook it out.*
Young Nehemiah	*This is how God will shake any of you who don't keep your promise. God will take away your houses and everything you own, and will leave you with nothing.*
Old Nehemiah	*Everyone who was present said:*
Women 1 & 2 *Men 1 & 2* *Leaders 1 & 2*	*AMEN!*
Old Nehemiah	*And praised the Lord. And the leaders kept their promise.*

Briefly, the group can move into three teams, Nehemiah, the ordinary people, and the leaders, to discuss these questions.

- What are your feelings?

- How do your feelings change at different stages of the story?

- Why does everyone manage to agree at the end?

Nehemiah recalled the people, especially the leaders, to the proper stewardship of the land. He saw that when ordinary people have too little power, they lose their contact with the land, they lose their security of housing and work, they risk becoming slaves, they get into hopeless debt, they have value only as producers of wealth for the benefit of the rich. On the other hand, the rich decide how much anything is worth, especially how much any land is worth, because they have the spare wealth to pay for it.

So Nehemiah called a mass meeting. He acknowledged that he himself was part of the problem: he and other leaders had become implicated in a system which was destroying the unity of God's community. He proposed the abolition of the present system of land–tenure, without compensation.

He saw that poverty was not an accident, nor was it primarily the fault of the poor: it was caused by a long series of decisions made by the powerful. For him, as political and religious leader, to be neutral in such a situation would mean taking the side of the wealthy and abandoning the justice of God.

PRACTICAL PLANNING

Does this seem like a different world from twentieth–century Britain? Is this all old irrelevant legislation? What possible connection can there be with our calling to be stewards in today's Church?

1. However different our circumstances may be now, surely we ought not to be willing to put up with a social system which is any less just and equitable than the arrangements of the law of Moses. All people cannot have a small holding of their own: but a just society will be one in which everyone has a share in the wealth which is created through possession of the land. The old rating system was a somewhat crude way of doing this. Are any of your church members involved in the debate about local authority taxation?

2. How satisfied are you with your church's stewardship of its land? Do you know how decisions are taken about the disposal of Church land and assets on sale? How do you feel about Church property and Church land being virtually idle, or used for only a few hours a month, when in some areas there is real homelessness?

3. What do you feel about the apparent success of Nehemiah's ruling? Why were people evidently content to surrender some of their wealth? How did he get their consent?

- Why do we pay taxes — taxes which to some extent serve the same purpose? Of course, there is a compulsory system, and we do not find it easy to get round PAYE and VAT. But, fundamentally, our tax system depends on consent. It won't work unless there is some degree of public will to make it work. So, what about such a matter as housing for the poorer members of our nation? For twenty years, we have been able to move small cargoes of individuals across the world at speeds faster than the speed of sound. We have got the technology, the skills, and the finance to produce Concorde: we surely have the technology, the skills, and the finance to beat the housing problem. The one thing missing seems to be the will, the motive to get the job done. And that is entirely a spiritual matter. We, as the Church, are stewards of spiritual resources for the working out of God's will. How then is God's will to work today in our country with this long–standing problem?

UNIT 5 LABOUR

GETTING STARTED

To work means being a steward of energy and skill. So see what work is about, for you.

- What are the occupations of the members of your group?

- What sort of hours do you work?

- How long does it take you to get to work and back?

- For you, is there a clear difference between work and leisure?

- Who benefits from your work, and how?

DIGGING DEEPER

DEUTERONOMY 5.6–21

I am the LORD your God who brought you out of Egypt, out of that land where you lived as slaves.

You must have no other gods beside me.

You are not to make a carved image for yourself, nor the likeness of anything in the heavens above, or on the earth below, or in the waters under the earth. You must not worship or serve them: for I am the LORD your God, a jealous God, punishing children for the sins of their parents to the third and fourth generations of those who reject me. But I keep faith with thousands, those who love me and keep my commandments. You shall not make wrong use of the name of the LORD your God; the LORD will not leave unpunished anyone who misuses his name.

Observe the Sabbath day and keep it holy as the LORD your God commanded you. You have six days to labour and do all your work; but the seventh day is a Sabbath of the LORD your God; that day you must not do any work, neither you, nor your son or your daughter, your slave or your slave–girl, your ox, your donkey, or any of your cattle, or the alien residing among you, so that your slaves and slave–girls may rest as you do. Bear in mind that you were slaves in Egypt, and the LORD your God brought you out with a strong hand and an outstretched arm, and for that reason the LORD your God has commanded you to keep the Sabbath day.

Honour your father and your mother, as the LORD your God commanded you, so that you may enjoy long life, and it will be well with you in the land which the LORD your God is giving you.

Do not commit murder.

Do not commit adultery.

Do not steal.

Do not give baseless evidence against your neighbour.

Do not lust after your neighbour's wife; do not covet your neighbour's household, his land, his slave, his slave–girl, his ox, his donkey, or anything that belongs to him.

There are three forms of wealth in the law of Moses, and they all come directly under God's will and God's scrutiny. The first is land. The second is labour. (The third, learning, is dealt with in Unit 6.)

The opening sentence reminds us that we are liberated slaves, and the longest verse regulates our labour so that we will not become slaves again. Every one of the commandments is designed to help the community hold together: what is forbidden is the whole array of things which cause communities to fragment in resentment and distrust — partisanship, divisiveness, economy with the truth, theft of property, theft of life, of good name, of domestic stability. The Sabbath law is, primarily, a labour law. For one day each week, the distinctions of labour are put aside; for one day in seven, people who are otherwise in categories of employer, employee, and unemployed, are united in rest and freedom. If you don't observe this law, you are likely to become slaves all over again. As slaves, you had a kind of equality because none of you had a voice, none of you had any rights, you were all valued solely as producers for someone else's profit. Now that you are free, make sure you don't fall into a new slavery based on inequalities among yourselves.

What the Israelites had experienced was the slavery of being in bondage as a whole nation to another nation, as blacks were slaves of whites not so long ago. Now the new danger was that members of the same nation would be enslaved to each other. And the mechanism of this enslavement was debt. So the seventh year, the Sabbath year, was a time for remission of debts. Debts would be incurred, in the ordinary ups and downs of life, but they must not be permanent. The rich are not to live permanently on interest paid by the poor.

LEVITICUS 25.35–43

If your brother–Israelite is reduced to poverty and cannot support himself in the community, you must assist him as you would an alien or a stranger, and he will live with you. You must not charge him interest on a loan, either by deducting it in advance from the capital sum, or by adding it on repayment. Fear your God, and let your brother live with you; do not deduct interest when advancing him money, or add interest to the payment due for food supplied on credit. I am the LORD *your God who brought you out of Egypt to give you Canaan and to become your God.*

If your fellow–countryman is reduced to poverty and sells himself to you, you must not use him to work for you as a slave. His status will be that of a hired man or a stranger lodging with you: he will work for you only until the jubilee year. He will then leave your service, with his children, and go back to his family and to his ancestral property: because they are my slaves whom I brought out of Egypt, they must not be sold as slaves are sold. You must not work him ruthlessly, but you are to fear your God.

We note again, that the law of God carries with it its own motive. "I the LORD your God have set you free, therefore..." Our dealing with our neighbour is our response to God. Neglect of the Sabbath is totally bound up with exploitation of the poor.

It is a kind of sickness in the community when debt is allowed to rule. It traps people so that they cannot make responsible decisions and take initiatives of their own. So this law seeks to ensure that indebtedness does not become a person's permanent condition.

The Old Testament attitude to slavery was unique in the laws of those days. Other cultures had codes of conduct for such matters as civil disputes. But Israel had remarkable regulations regarding compensation for injury to a slave by a master, and providing for asylum for runaway slaves (Exodus 21.26–27; Deuteronomy 23.15–16). The law actually commanded protection for slaves. It is easy for us to criticize St Paul on account of his apparent toleration of slavery; but he was in this same tradition, when he, unlike other writers of his day, addressed slaves as morally responsible individuals, members of the body of Christ (e.g. Colossians 3.22–25).

Israel's land laws were designed to prevent the division of society into a small number of landowners and a large number of landless people (see Unit 4). Her labour laws were designed to prevent the division of society into a small number of people making all the decisions and a large number simply contributing servile muscle power.

Most nations celebrate their heroes and past triumphs. Israel was different. She did not allow herself to forget that, as a nation, she started off as a rabble of escaped slaves. She knew God first and foremost as a God who is on the side of slaves and wills them to be free. So, if society gets divided into those whose work is controlled and those who control them, God is likely to be on the side of the former. Similarly, if there were aliens in society, the Israelites were not to oppress or exploit them: "You yourselves know how it feels to be aliens, because you were aliens in Egypt" (Exodus 23.9).

The command to "love the alien" is one which runs right through the Bible. It is repeated several times in the law of Moses (Exodus 22.21; Leviticus 19.33–34; Deuteronomy 27.19). In the prophets, God is seen working through those who are outside Israel's community (Isaiah 44.28); he claims her enemies as communities through whom the world is to be blessed (Isaiah 19.23–25). Jesus shows that love of the enemy is the most significant test of love (Matthew 5.43–48).

And, in his last and most decisive parable, he shows that the final judgement on a nation will depend on its attitude to those who are outside its main communities (Matthew 25.31–46). The most important moral judgement on the Church, therefore, would not be with regard to its internal fellowship, its worship or doctrine: it would be concerning its attitude to those outside its community. This has to be a crucial question to the Church today as it examines its stewardship.

PRACTICAL PLANNING

Labour is a basis of wealth, and therefore of our responsibility as stewards of God's resources. Among the people of God, everyone should be able to use skills and energies that God has given.

- What resources of skill and experience do you have in your group or your church?

  Are they being fully used?

  Are they being exploited in such a way that people feel enslaved?

- How much scope is there for the contribution of the "outsider", the "alien", the person who doesn't easily fit into the tradition, the newcomer?

  How far are you able to give responsibility, roles or tasks to, for instance, those who are newly confirmed?

- How far does your worship bring people together so that their differences of role in society (employer and employee etc.) are truly overcome?

- Do you look back with pride at your achievements, or is there some kind of deliverance to which you can look back in celebration and thanksgiving?

- Are there ways in which your church can influence attitudes and practice with regard to employment and unemployment in your area?

- What does all this have to say to us who live in a land where increasing numbers of people have debt problems, where many are becoming homeless through repossession?

- And what does this say to us when so many poor countries are having to spend almost all their foreign exchange on servicing debts? Some major banks seem to feel that this indebtedness is such a block on economic development that they cancel debts not out of compassion but as a remedy for economic sickness. How can we contribute to public awareness and policy on these matters? How far are we involved in the educational (as opposed to the fundraising) work of bodies like Christian Aid?

- "Love the stranger." Can you say that your church lives according to this rule? Can you say that your nation lives according to this rule? What should be done about this?

UNIT 6   LEARNING

GETTING STARTED

Compare notes with each other about the age at which you left full–time education.

- What subjects did you find most interesting?

- What subjects would you like to take further, if you had the chance?

- Do you in fact have the chance now? Could you study the subjects which you are interested in at a local College of Further Education, through the W.E.A. or the Open University? Has the Church something for you in its Adult Education programme? Have you tried to find out?

DIGGING DEEPER

DEUTERONOMY 31. 9–13

Moses wrote down this law and gave it to the priests, the sons of Levi, who carried the Ark of the Covenant of the Lord, and to all the elders of Israel. Moses gave them this command: at the end of every seven years, at the appointed time for the year of remission, at the pilgrim–feast of Booths, when all Israel comes to appear before the Lord your God in the place which he will choose, this law is to be read in the hearing of all Israel. Assemble the people: men, women and dependants, together with the aliens residing in your settlements, so that they may listen, and learn to fear the Lord your God and observe all these laws with care. Their children, too, who do not know the laws, will hear them, and learn to fear the Lord your God all their lives in the land which you will occupy after crossing the Jordan.

According to the law of Moses, there are three basic sources of wealth. The first two are land and labour. Now we come to the third, learning.

This paragraph comes very near the end of the last book of the law, Deuteronomy. The law of God has been spelled out, in considerable detail. It has been covering all kinds of subjects, civil and criminal law, medicine, environmental concerns, history, liturgy, sanitation, dietetics, census studies, natural science, marriage and family regulations, children's issues, social welfare, employment, working conditions, the rights of aliens, animal welfare, and so on. Finally comes the provision for all this knowledge to be shared and implemented by the whole community. The Sabbath year is to be a year not only of rest and of worship, but also a year of education. The Levites have the task of ensuring that no one is ignorant. Society is not to be divided into a small group of experts and a large mass of irresponsible serfs. In our culture, it is the top people on the educational ladder who get the privilege of a sabbatical year, to enable them to climb higher. In the law of Israel the sabbatical year is a space to enable every citizen, including children, to catch up with all the knowledge that the law represents. This is education for justice. Knowledge is not restricted to those who can pay for it. Everybody is to be able to share intelligently in God's work. This underlies the vision of the prophet Jeremiah, that, in the new Covenant, there will be no specialist experts in the knowledge of God, because knowledge will be completely shared. The obstruction to knowledge is not just ignorance but the unforgiven guilt which divides person from person and group from group (Jeremiah 31.31–34).

Where the law is truly known and is the common property of the people, everyone has a stake in the integrity of the law, and the general public can be on their guard against bad practice. So we get the instructions in Exodus 23:1–9, where everyone is told how to behave if they find themselves in the roles of witness, adversary, or judge. Typically, this passage reminds the people that they also know what it is like to have no legal rights, because they were aliens in Egypt: and it leads on into yet another reminder about the Sabbath principle for land and labour.

However good the law may be, if people are powerless, if they are ignorant of their rights, if they are too poor or illiterate to know their way around the law, they can be hurt as much by the processes of good law as by bad law or by flagrant injustice. But where there is conscientious and generous stewardship of that most precious and sometimes most secret commodity, knowledge, then people can feel that the law is truly on their side and God is on their side. So knowledge leads to praise, to the kind of delight in

God's law which is expressed throughout Psalm 119: "Your instruction is my continual delight; I turn to it for counsel." (Verse 24.) "I shall run the course made known in your commandments, for you set free my heart." (Verse 32.)

We need to be warned by the experience of Jesus, who found that the stewards of the law in his day were making the Sabbath a restriction instead of a blessing. This is the danger, when the stewards of the things of God are more interested in their own security than in making the blessings of God's gifts available to everyone. The Gospel of Christ is that the Son of Man is Lord of the Sabbath, so that the freedom and healing represented by the Sabbath can flow (Mark 2.27–28).

PRACTICAL PLANNING

- How well do you think your church is working as a steward of knowledge?

- What sort of adult education programme does it provide? How far are ministers able to share the knowledge which they have been given?

- What place does education for children and young people have in your church's budget?

- What opportunities do members have to share with each other their experiences of struggle, of exploration, of discovery, in the meaning of their faith in the context of their ordinary work?

- What opportunities for "second–chance" education are there in your area?

- What contacts are there between the church and your local college of Further Education? Are there opportunities for cooperation?

- Are some of your members involved in organizations like Citizens Advice Bureaus, which help people to know and claim their rights under the law?

SECTION C
THE MINISTRY OF JESUS

UNIT 7 A MIRACLE OF SALVATION

GETTING STARTED

Divide the following passage into characters (everyone can take the part of the "Grumbling Person" if you like), and read it aloud.

JESUS AND ZACCHAEUS
Luke 19.1–10
(From *The Dramatised Bible*)

Narrator	*Jesus went on into Jericho and was passing through. There was a chief tax collector there named Zacchaeus, who was rich. He was trying to see who Jesus was, but he was a little man and could not see Jesus because of the crowd. So he ran ahead of the crowd and climbed a sycamore tree to see Jesus, who was going to pass that way. When Jesus came to that place, he looked up.*
Jesus	*Hurry down, Zacchaeus, because I must stay in your house today.*
Narrator	*Zacchaeus hurried down and welcomed him with great joy.*
	(Pause)
	All the people who saw it started grumbling:
Grumbling person	*This man has gone as a guest to the home of a sinner!*
Narrator	*Zacchaeus stood up [and said to the Lord]:*

Zacchaeus (to Jesus)	*Listen, sir! I will give half my belongings to the poor, and if I have cheated anyone, I will pay him back four times as much.*
Jesus (to Zacchaeus)	*Salvation has come to this house today, for this man, also, is a descendant of Abraham. The Son of Man came to seek and to save the lost.*

Now discuss the following questions:

- What interests you in this story?

- Who do you sympathize with?

- Who is the shortest person in your group?

- What does he or she feel like in a crowd?

DIGGING DEEPER

In Unit 2, we noticed how, in the history of the people of the Bible, taxation had changed from the just system of the law of Moses to the oppressive system of Palestine in the days of Jesus.

The basic idea of the law of Moses was that God had set his people free. Therefore they treated each other justly, shared the wealth produced from the land, prevented the land from being held by a small number of people in large estates, and operated a tax system to care for people who had no land–rights. We might ask was this just a dream, or was it practical politics? It seems that, centuries after the law of Moses was written, the Jewish people were a community of free families with smallholdings. When they were conquered by Greeks, they fought for their religious faith because their faith was the basis of their system of land–tenure, and therefore of their personal freedom. Their law was based on their gospel.

But by the time that Jesus was living, this system had collapsed. Peasants were forced to work for absentee landlords in order to earn the money for rent, and for the tax which had to be paid to the Roman colonial power. Strictly speaking, the Romans did not employ tax collectors. They sold the right to collect taxes to private operators: these tax collectors had a target–figure of money which they were expected to pay to their masters. They themselves decided how much they would demand from any individual peasant. Provided they sent on the required amount to their masters, they could extract what they liked from the peasants. For a peasant who could not stand the system, the only solution was to go up into the hills and become a brigand. It's a pattern which can be seen all over the world where colonial methods prevail.

We could express it in a diagram:

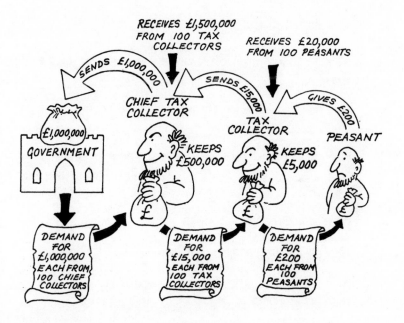

Zacchaeus fitted securely into this system. He was a chief tax–collector. Typically, he was a native, with a Hebrew name, but had adapted his name to fit the language of his foreign masters. He didn't belong anywhere. In the eyes of the Jewish leaders, people like him had cut themselves off from their own people, and were no longer members of the family of Abraham. They were as good as dead. He had separated himself from the people of the land, and had climbed into a little nest of individual private wealth.

Divide your group into three teams, to look imaginatively at the different characters.

---

1. Jesus

   What are you doing here — in Jericho?

   Where have you come from?

   Where are you going?

   What are the problems which you face as you decide what to do about Zacchaeus?

2. The crowd, the disciples

   What is your opinion of Jesus at the beginning of the story?

   How does your opinion change during the course of the story?

   What do you think about the various stages in the story?

3. Zacchaeus

   What do you really want?

   What change happens to you in the course of the story?

   What are you actually doing when you make your decisions about money at the end of the story, and why?

   (If you have enough people for a fourth team, you could have a team for the storyteller, Luke. Why do you tell the story? What use do you think it is going to be for your friends in the Church for which you are writing? What do you think you mean by the special word "Salvation" in Jesus' last statement?)

When the teams have had time to feel their way into the characters of the story, they can learn from each other by sending one or two representatives to each other. The Jesus team can send one or two members to the Crowd team. The Crowd team can send one or two members to the Zacchaeus team. The Zacchaeus team can send one or two members to the Jesus team. (The Luke team can break up and observe the other three teams.)

In each case, the visiting members start off the conversation by asking this question to the team they are visiting: "What is the problem which I am causing you?"

After a few minutes, the teams meet together as one group and share their findings.

Some points to note.

1. Realize what a horrible person Zacchaeus is. For a long time Jesus has been trying to help the poor peasants to feel that God is interested in them: he has been taking the side of people who get little advantage from society. Here, almost at the end of his journey to Jerusalem, he puts all this at risk by associating himself with this rich man.

2. Notice the commands of Jesus, formulated very precisely for specific needs (Mark 2.11; Mark 5.41; Mark 7.34; Mark 9.25; Luke 17.14 etc.). Zacchaeus is given a very exact instruction "Come down." That is to say, stop putting yourself at a distance from the rest of us — your salvation is not in being separate but by rejoining the rest of us in our poverty.

3. Zacchaeus responds because Jesus puts himself at risk, invites himself into this horrible man's house and accepts his hospitality.

4. Zacchaeus forfeits half his capital wealth to the poor, the landless peasants. He also imposes upon himself the maximum fine for theft, in both Roman and Jewish law. He gives to the poor not in generosity but in justice. He restores to the poor what was all the time truly theirs.

5. All this adds up to "salvation". Jesus does not simply tell Zacchaeus that he is saved, he gives Zacchaeus an experience which conveys the meaning of salvation. In spite of his behaviour, Zacchaeus has not, in fact, been cut off from the people of God. His security is guaranteed, not by his moral standing but by the reckless generosity of Jesus.

6. This is a story of a miracle. Zacchaeus is spiritually, economically, and socially sick. His healing is just as miracu-
lous as the healing of the paralytic or the blind. For such a
person to be restored to wholeness was, according to the
religious leaders of the time, as improbable as the raising
of the dead.

At the end of this phase, it would be useful to read the story again,
with appropriate movement. At one end of the room is the tree,
with Zacchaeus alone. At the other end is Jesus with the crowd.
Jesus calls Zacchaeus to him. Zacchaeus comes. Now the crowd
can ask themselves: "What are we going to do?" Either they stay
put, with Jesus and Zacchaeus; or they move away from
Zacchaeus, and from Jesus, to the other end of the room by the
tree. If they draw the line at Zacchaeus, they draw the line at Jesus.

Luke gave us this story because he knew that the Church would
need it in order to continue Christ's way of responding to people.
There would be new Zacchaeuses in new situations. Would the
Church respond in the manner of the crowd or in the manner of
Jesus?

PRACTICAL PLANNING

- Who do you think might be Zacchaeus for us, in our area
  now? How should the Church, as the body of Christ, act
  towards such a person?

- Are we quite clear that our giving away of money is a
  response to God's generosity to us, and not just an obedience to a rule? How can we ensure that we represent this
  principle properly in stewardship programmes?

- The notion of stewardship will work properly only when
  wealth has been genuinely entrusted to us. It will not work
  for wealth which, like the wealth of Zacchaeus, has in
  effect been stolen. What do you think of these three quotations from some of the great early teachers of the Church?

  "The bread in your cupboard
  belongs to the hungry man;
  The coat hanging unused in
  your closet belongs to the

*man who needs it; the shoes
rotting in your closet
belong to the man who has no
shoes; the money which you put
in the bank belongs to the poor." (St Basil)*

*"Do not say, 'I am using what
belongs to me.' You are using
what belongs to others. All the
wealth of the world belongs to
you and to others in common,
as the sun, air, earth, and all
the rest." (St Chrysostom)*

*"In giving to the poor, we are
returning to them what is theirs
by right, for the earth is our
common property." (St Ambrose)*

- Now consider this statement:

  "The question to be asked is not what we should give to the poor but when we will stop taking from the poor. The poor are not our problem: we are their problem." (Jim Wallis, *The Call to Conversion,* Lion, 1981.)

- Do you agree with it?

  If so, is it, for you, a threatening bit of logic, or is it some kind of vision of freedom, something to do with the love of God for you? And, if this sort of motive really works for you, how can you put it across, for instance, in the motivation for Christian Aid week?

UNIT 8   TALENT-SPOTTING

INTRODUCTION

We turn now to look at some of the teaching of Jesus about stewardship. He did not, in fact, have a great deal to say about stewardship in the most exact sense of the word, but he did have a good deal to say about money. And much of what he had to say about stewardship is in the form of parables.

When Jesus used parables, he was not always trying to give a specific moral lesson. Often his intention was to make people work out something for themselves, to make them think. He would tell a provocative story to disturb their assumptions and their certainties and, in effect, asked them: "With whom do you identify in this story? Where do you fit into it? What does it teach you about yourself and your possibilities?" (The most obvious example of this is the Parable of the Good Samaritan in Luke 10.25–37.) This uncovers an aspect of the gospel, the Good News, which is always something of a surprise. So don't be disappointed if at first you find yourself saying: "I don't see what he's getting at" — there may well be more than one answer.

GETTING STARTED

During the days leading up to this meeting, let every member of the group watch out for signs on the media, of what are referred to as "talents".

- What is meant by a "talented" child?

- Who decides on this meaning?

- Whose expectations are being met by a child or adult who is called "talented"?

DIGGING DEEPER

JESUS TELLS THE STORY OF THE GOLD COINS
Luke 19.12–13, 15–26
(From *The Dramatised Bible*)

[Narrator   *Jesus told them a parable. He was now almost at Jerusalem, and they supposed that the Kingdom of God was just about to appear. So he said:*]

Jesus   *There was once a man of high rank who was going to a country far away to be made king, after which he planned to come back home. Before he left, he called his ten servants and gave them each a gold coin and told them:*

King   *See what you can earn with this while I am gone.*

Jesus   *The man was made king and came back. At once he ordered his servants to appear before him, in order to find out how much they had earned. The first one came and said:*

Servant 1   *Sir, I have earned ten gold coins with the one you gave me.*

King
(to Servant 1)   *Well done, you are a good servant! Since you were faithful in small matters, I will put you in charge of ten cities.*

Jesus   *The second servant came and said:*

Servant 2   *Sir, I have earned five gold coins with the one you gave me.*

King
(to Servant 2)   *You will be in charge of five cities.*

Jesus   *Another servant came and said:*

Servant 3   *Sir, here is your gold coin; I kept it hidden in a handkerchief. I was afraid of you, because you are a hard man. You take what is not yours and reap what you did not sow.*

King (to Servant 3)	You bad servant! I will use your own words to condemn you! You know that I am a hard man, taking what is not mine and reaping what I have not sown. Well, then, why didn't you put my money in the bank? Then I would have received it back with interest when I returned.
Jesus	Then he said to those who were standing there:
King	Take the gold coin away from him and give it to the servant who has ten coins.
[Jesus	But they said to him:]
Person	Sir, he already has ten coins!
Jesus	The king replied:
King	I tell you, that to every person who has something, even more will be given; but the person who has nothing, even the little that he has will be taken away from him.

Divide into three teams.
Team A takes the part of the king.
Team B takes the part of the first and second servants.
Team C takes the part of the third servant.
Each team tries to get into the feelings and role of the character(s) it represents. Use your imagination.

You could use these questions to help you to do this:

• What sort of people are we?

• What is our main aim?

• What motives are most important for us in this situation?

• What is our opinion about the other characters in the story?

After ten minutes or so, each team should choose one or two of its members to go to represent it in conversation with another team. A delegate goes from each team to visit one other team. A delegation from team B (servants 1 and 2) goes to team C (servant 3). A delegation from team C (servant 3) goes to team A (the king). A delegation from team A (the king) goes to team B (servants 1 and 2).

In each case, the visiting delegation asks the host team:

- What do you think of me/us?

- Are we all going to be able to have anything to do with each other in the future?

Then after a few minutes' conversation, the delegates go back to their original teams and exchange experiences.

Through this process, you will have got into the parable which Jesus told. Now you need to discover what Jesus was trying to do to his audience by telling this parable: and what the parable is intended to mean for us in our stewardship.

So, now continue in the three teams, but look at the whole story as an event in Jesus' work.

Team A takes on the character of Jesus.

Team B takes on the character of the disciples.

Team C takes on the character of Luke, the storyteller who has passed the whole story on to us.

Team A, Jesus, should tackle the questions:

- Why am I telling this parable?

- What am I aiming at?

- What effect do I hope this parable will have on my hearers?

Team B, the disciples, should tackle the questions:

- What is Jesus up to?

- What do we feel that the parable is saying to us?

> • Where do we fit into the story?
>
> Team C, Luke, should tackle the questions:
>
> • Why do I think that this parable is worth passing on to my readers?
>
> • What good is it going to do for the church I am writing for?

When the teams have had time to explore these questions, they should come together in one large group and share their answers.

Notice verse 11. Jesus tells the parable in order to correct a misunderstanding about timing. People think that, because things are looking good, there is nothing further that needs to be done. They hope that time will stop at the point where they receive good fortune, they want to keep things as they are. Those who have done well in the immediate past often have a decisive influence on a nation's political and social life. But the gift which Jesus gives does not bring history to a stop. The gift has to be used: there is still a need for adventure and risk and new work. Our assets are given to us to use, to put to work, not to preserve, parade, or hide.

We have to make the most of the time that we are given. The coin hidden in a napkin survives, but it does not grow; it is no use until it is used.

The coins belong to the master: they are only lent to the servants. All the servants correctly speak to the master of "your coin". The "gifts" which are given are not for the servants' benefit but to help forward the master's work.

All are put to the same work, all receive the same amount. Much the same applies in the Parable of the Talents (Matthew 25.14–30 — a story which is different in several important ways, but teaches much the same lesson). No one is given no talent, but the person who behaves as if he has been given no talent will end up with no talent.

The coins, or talents, therefore, are not personal abilities, which are ours to use as we please. A talent is, in the first place, something on loan to us to use for God. We need to check how far we are bending the word away from its true meaning, when we talk about "having a talent" for, say, breeding poodles. Unless the talent is being put to use for the purposes for God's kingdom, it isn't a talent, it's just a skill like any other.

Often, in practice, children are called talented when they seem to be able to gain more rewards for themselves as individuals in a competitive system. Those who start off with advantages are enabled to move up into greater advantage, leaving others behind. This may be all part of the way of the world, but it usually has got little to do with the idea that the talent is lent by God for the purposes of God's kingdom.

The reward for faithfulness in the use of the coin or the talent is not more money but greater responsibility.

Stewardship is like a bicycle, with a front wheel called Adventure and a rear wheel called Efficiency. Adventure means risk, trying out new opportunities. Efficiency is really another word for obedience, because it means efficiency in serving the purposes which are specified by the master. Any true Christian stewardship needs to run on both these two wheels. And this leads us into our practical planning.

PRACTICAL PLANNING

There are many possibilities here and you may prefer to divide again into the small teams to consider them. But first, two general points.

A. There is opportunity later in the course to go into detail about finance; this unit is not mainly about finance and you would miss some other important aspects of stewardship if you were to get deep into finance at this point.

B. As individual Christians we should all, of course, be good stewards of our own personal resources. But we will do this best if we can see that the Church as a community is treating its own stewardship as a combination of efficiency and adventure. So, start with some questions on the following lines:

---

1. What is the "talent" which we, as the Church community, have been entrusted with in this place? Are we preserving it, are we using it, are we risking it so that it can grow?

The Church also has particular "talents" to use:

2. We have people, with a lot of different skills, abilities, and experiences?

- How far do we know what resources of this kind we have? Could we be making better use of them, by a little more conscious planning? How carefully, for instance, are the members of our church council and its committees chosen?

- How well does our church use its ministers? Do they feel that they are able to give all that they should be giving? Is the church helping them to be efficient and to improve their skills?

- How far are our members able to use and share their experience — for instance, their experience of conflict, of struggle with unbelief, of bereavement, of sickness, of parenthood, of other cultures and languages, etc.?

3. We have time. In particular, our time together on Sundays is a gift of God.

- How well are we using this time, in service of God's purposes? When was our programme for Sundays last reviewed, and on what basis are decisions made about the programme? Could we grow better by having, on occasion, a longer time of fellowship on a Sunday?

- What about our ecumenical resources? Taken as a whole, is the Sunday programme of the Christian organizations of your area either efficient or adventurous?

- What about other opportunities for good use of time?

4. We have buildings and equipment.

- Are we using them as a "talent"? Are they things to use or things only to preserve?

- Is our stewardship in this area efficient and adventurous?

5. To whom is your church accountable? When, as a church, do you feel you are being required to give an account of your stewardship?

With questions of this sort in mind, individual members can be encouraged to continue their own personal self–assessment. Each member, however young or old, has his or her abilities, experiences, and opportunities. These are all part of our stewardship, and all need to be made part of our offertory. For instance, do you live in a house or flat next door to other people? Isn't that, in itself, a "talent"?

- You have 168 hours each week; make a list of the various ways in which you spent those hours last week. Do you feel called to change that pattern at all? Have you worked out what you mean by "leisure", and in some way is this part of your "talent"?

- Do you have opportunities to shape public opinion — not necessarily by making big speeches but by the way you respond in day–to–day conversation? Do you have opportunity to oppose misunderstanding and prejudices about Christ and the Church, about peace and justice, about people who suffer disadvantage in our society? Are you making use of this "talent" — and is the Church helping you to respond to this sort of opportunity?

- You have your own personal history — you belong in a particular family, you speak a particular language, you share in a particular part of society, you have been formed by a particular kind of education etc. Are you able to see all this sort of thing as a "talent", as something to use for God's purposes? Or is it merely a whole lot of defences against other people?

- What other "talents" do you have, which you can offer, either through the church or through some other way?

The members of the group should go away and think personally about this sort of question. Perhaps each person can try to come back next time with one new way in which a "talent" can be offered to God and claimed for God's purposes.

Finally, as a group, you would set yourself a task of working out a method by which the talents of members can be offered and celebrated in an act of worship, perhaps in an extended form of the preparation of the gifts at the Eucharist.

UNIT 9   TWO PARABLES

GETTING STARTED

Is any member of the group able to tell a story of personal experience on the lines of "How I learned from my mistake"? It needn't be a very soul–searching story; but other members of the group should understand how the mistake came to be made and how it could be put right.

When you have listened to the story, consider these questions:

- Can the mistake be put right?

- Who can put it right, the person who made the mistake, or someone else, such as the person in charge?

- What are the costs involved in putting it right? Who loses and who gains?

DIGGING DEEPER

JESUS TELLS TWO PARABLES
Parable A: Luke 12.22, 35–48
(From *The Dramatised Bible*)

Narrator	*Jesus said to the disciples:*
Jesus	*Be ready for whatever comes, dressed for action and with your lamps lit, like servants who are waiting for their master to come back from a wedding feast. When he comes and knocks, they will open the door for him at once. How happy are those servants whose master finds them awake and ready when he returns! I tell you, he will take off his coat, ask them to sit down, and will wait on them. How happy they are if he finds them ready, even if he should come at midnight or even later! And you can be sure that if the owner of a house knew the time when the thief would come, he would not let the thief break into his house. And you, too, must be ready, because the Son of Man will come at an hour when you are not expecting him.*

Narrator	Peter said:
Peter	Lord does this parable apply to us, or do you mean it for everyone?
Narrator	The Lord answered:
Jesus	Who, then, is the faithful and wise servant? He is the one that his master will put in charge, to run the household and give the other servants their share of the food at the proper time. How happy that servant is if his master finds him doing this when he comes home! Indeed, I tell you, the master will put that servant in charge of all his property. But if that servant says to himself that his master is taking a long time to come back and if he begins to beat the other servants, both the men and the women, and eats and drinks and gets drunk, then the master will come back one day when the servant does not expect him and at a time he does not know. The master will cut him in pieces and make him share the fate of the disobedient.
	The servant who knows what his master wants him to do, but does not get himself ready and do it, will be punished with a heavy whipping. But the servant who does not know what his master wants, and yet does something for which he deserves a whipping, will be punished with a light whipping. Much is required from the person to whom much is given; much more is required from the person to whom much more is given.

Parable B: Luke 16.1–8
(From *The Dramatised Bible*)

Jesus	There was once a rich man who had a servant who managed his property. The rich man was told that the manager was wasting his master's money, so he called him in.
Master	What is this I hear about you? Present me with a complete account of your handling of my property, because you cannot be my manager any longer.
Jesus	The servant said to himself:

Manager	My master is going to dismiss me from my job. What shall I do? I am not strong enough to dig ditches, and I am ashamed to beg. Now I know what I will do! Then when my job is gone, I shall have friends who will welcome me in their homes.
Jesus	So he called in all the people who were in debt to his master. He asked the first one:
Manager (to Debtor)	How much do you owe my master?
Debtor 1	One hundred barrels of olive oil.
Jesus	The manager told him:
Manager	Here is your account; sit down and write fifty.
[Jesus	Then he asked another one:]
Manager (to Debtor 2)	And you — how much do you owe?
Debtor 2	A thousand sacks of wheat.
Manager	Here is your account, write eight hundred.
Jesus	As a result the master of this dishonest manager praised him for doing such a shrewd thing; because the people of this world are much more shrewd in handling their affairs than the people who belong to the light.

Stewards are employees. Their task is to look after the household of the employer. In Jesus' day a steward was often a slave who himself owned nothing. Perhaps the most accurate title would be "Household Manager". The steward is, literally, the "economy–person". In the New Testament the word economy means both the administration of God's household and the "hidden purpose" of God's plan (Ephesians 1.10 and 3.9). The steward, therefore, is required not merely to carry out orders; the steward has to be committed to the purpose and the plan, and can be relied on not to prefer his or her own private ambitions. As employees, stewards always face the possibility of redundancy or dismissal for incompetence.

The group should divide into two teams. Team A should look at the story of the "merciless" steward of Luke Chapter 12 and Team B at the story of the "dishonest" steward of Luke Chapter 16.

Team A. Look at the whole passage from the point of view of the servant who was raised to the rank of steward (give him a name). He had been very conscientious, so much so that his master had actually given him a dinner and had waited on him. He had been given responsibility for the whole household; this responsibility meant caring for all the members of the household and seeing to their well–being. But he started to take his master's absence for granted; he started to treat the place as his own, to serve his own hunger for power. He became domineering over his subordinates and exploited them. This behaviour was totally different from the ways of the master; the way the steward ran the household gave a completely. false impression of the master's nature. So the master is furious and that is the end of the steward.

By the end of your time in the team you should be able to tell this steward's story of "How I lost my job."

Team B. Look at the whole passage from the point of view of the steward in this story (give him a name). This steward's main responsibility was not for subordinate employees but for the rents and other revenues of an absentee landlord. He had been using his master's assets to enrich himself by lending them out at high interest rates and taking the profit himself (this is what is meant by "squandering" the property — it's a situation which will be recognized as true to life by anyone who has lived in a colonial society such as Palestine was in the days of Jesus). When he realized that he was going to get the sack, he came to see that he was doing himself no good by enriching himself at the expense of the poor peasants around. So, he called in the bills, and deducted and abandoned the private profit which he had planned for himself. He ended up with no job, with nothing in his pocket, but enough goodwill among the poor peasants to keep himself in dinners and hospitality for the foreseeable future. His "dishonesty" was in the original misappropriation of his master's goods, for which he was called to account, not in his changing of the figures on the bills.

By the end of your time in the team you should be able to tell this steward's story of "How I lost my job."

The greatest danger for a steward is the temptation to misappropriate — to exploit things or people for one's own ends. All the steward has is someone else's: this is at the heart of Christian stewardship.

The first steward (Luke 12) felt confident that his master was a permanent absentee. This was the cause of his downfall and there was no second chance for him.

The second steward (Luke 16) went through a bad patch but then came to a moment of truth. He came to see that he would be better off as a welcome guest among the poor peasants than as an isolated rich man with no friends. He had thought that his problem was financial, a lack of money. In fact he came to see that there was a solution to his problem which didn't depend on getting money for himself; he started to control the financial system instead of being a victim of it. He became free.

The two teams should come together to tell each other their stories and compare notes.

Then the group should go back into the two teams; each team should consider its parable again, looking at it from the point of view of the disciples, the original hearers. They were mainly from the class of people represented by the subordinate servants in the first parable, and by the poor peasants in the second. So how would the disciples hear those parables? What would they feel about them? What would they think Jesus was intending by telling the stories — bearing in mind that he was training his disciples to take responsibilities as stewards? What was he getting at? Who was he getting at? For this stage, the teams could, if they wish, change over, Team A taking the story of the dishonest steward and Team B that of the merciless steward. (Note that, soon after hearing this teaching, according to Luke's timetable, the disciples had to cope with Jesus' action of accepting hospitality from a typical "unjust steward", eating with him, and declaring him "saved" — the story of Zacchaeus, Luke 19.1–10.)

The next stage is to ask: "Why did Luke, who had all sorts of material to select from, choose to include these two pieces of teaching? Why did he think that they would be useful in warning and inspiring his readers in the new Gentile churches?" Clearly, the same problems of irresponsible stewardship must have been a worry to Luke and his readers, otherwise there would have been no point in treasuring and communicating these parables.

And finally, the questions for us, in our day, arise:

- To whom is Jesus telling this story today?
- Whom is it aimed at?
- What dangers is it pointing out in our own church life?

One general point is, perhaps, that, if you exploit things you may be able to put it right: but if you exploit people, you may have passed the point of no return.

PRACTICAL PLANNING

Here are some points arising from the two parables:

Parable A: The merciless steward

---

1. We have been given a dinner by our master — we share in it at every Eucharist. But do we treat others in the way that we have been treated? Does the way in which we run

the household of the Church give a true or a misleading impression of the nature of our master? (This question needs to be answered by people who know what the Church looks like from outside.)

2. Do we in practice believe that we are accountable to God for the way our church is organized, or does it seem that God is, in effect, permanently absent and that we are getting on with it to satisfy our own ideas? Are we spending resources to satisfy our own tastes and preferences, rather than serving the purposes of Jesus?

3. We all have other people working for us, because we buy the products of other people's work. In many cases (for instance, when they are workers on tea or coffee plantations on the other side of the world), these people are treated very unfairly and we, as purchasers, are partly responsible for the poverty of their wages. Perhaps we are ignorant and deserve only a light beating (Luke 12.47–48). Or do some deserve a severe beating? If so, who?

Parable B: The dishonest steward

1. As a steward–church we have got all sorts of resources; are we using them to build relationships, to make friendships? Or are the things which we possess, as a church, separating us from other people and other groups? Are our possessions serving our basic purposes, or the other way round? Is it even possible that we might be better at making relationships if we were poorer? Might we do the really important work for God's kingdom better if we had fewer resources rather than if we had more? (Jesus, in Luke 12.48, points out the danger of possessing great resources — consider how the nations which have the greatest technological resources can also be the greatest threat to world peace.)

2. Do you think that our methods of dealing with money in the Church help or hinder our sense of fellowship? Do you find that some methods of fundraising make some people feel second–class citizens in the Church? Is there any gulf between people for whom money is a physical and tangible thing and those for whom money is represented by documents and signatures?

SECTION D
THE NEW TESTAMENT CHURCH

Units 10 to 12 are studies on chapters 8 and 9 of 2 Corinthians: the full text of these chapters is not printed here, so access to Bibles will be necessary.

UNIT 10   GENEROUS MACEDONIANS

GETTING STARTED

Think, for a minute or two, about what your blood is doing, right now. It moves around your body being renewed, being spent, and being sent back to the heart to be renewed again. It receives "wealth" as it rests in the lung–tissues, then goes out to spend itself in the other tissues, to love them as it has been loved. It is a device for keeping energy moving around, available where energy is needed.

In the body of a community, one of the things which helps to keep wealth moving around is money. Money is not itself wealth, in spite of our common way of talking. Money enables wealth, or energy, to be moved around, to take energy to where it is needed. It is a kind of life–blood of any large or scattered organization: it is very useful to the Church, and has been so from the earliest days of our movement. It has enabled wealth, or energy, or the ability to get things done, to be moved across distances and even across the seas.

DIGGING DEEPER

The longest and most detailed statement in the New Testament about the stewardship of money is in Paul's Second Letter to the Church in Corinth, Chapters 8 and 9. This is not a theoretical statement of principles, it is the story of a particular project and a particular appeal.

From the first day of our Christian movement, one of the distin-
guishing marks of the work of the Holy Spirit is the sharing of
wealth (Acts 2.44; 4.32–37). It is surely no accident that the gift of
the Holy Spirit (the "first–fruits" of God's purpose of restoring the
whole creation (Romans 8.23)) takes place on the Day of
Pentecost (Acts 2).

Pentecost was a festival of the first–fruits of the harvest, a festival recognizing God's claim on all wealth, a festival of sharing
across the boundaries of class and nation (Deuteronomy 16.9–12).
On the Day of Pentecost, the nations are gathered into one fellowship: and the community of God's people recognize God's claim
upon his creation and therefore each other's claim upon their
wealth.

A few years after the coming of the Holy Spirit at Pentecost, we
hear of the church in Antioch responding to a famine crisis by col-
lecting and sending money to the poorer church in Jerusalem (Acts
11.27–30).

The financial project in 2 Corinthians 8–9 is a natural development along the same lines. But it was, at the same time, something
very new. Antioch was after all only just down the road from
Jerusalem, and there would be many contacts between the two
cities. In sending money to Jerusalem from Greece and
Macedonia, the Church was making links between two groups of
people who were far apart and had very little in common. Roman
citizens would, of course, have a common bond with each other
across the Mediterranean world and beyond: but here was a movement which gave illiterate slaves in Corinth, righteous traditional-
ists in Jerusalem, and privileged citizens of Rome a sense that they
belonged together in one common wealth, with one equal status:
the one thing they had in common was the figure of Jesus. Nothing
like this had happened before.

If we are to understand Paul's appeal to the Church at Corinth,
first we need to see what happened at the Church in Macedonia.
Paul uses the Macedonian Church as his example of how poor
people can be inspired to help each other.

ACTS 16.10–40
(From *The Dramatised Bible*)

> Luke   As soon as Paul had this vision, we got ready
> to leave for Macedonia, because we decided
> that God had called us to preach the Good
> News to the people there.

We left by ship from Troas and sailed straight across to Samothrace, and the next day to Neapolis. From there we went inland to Philippi, a city of the first district of Macedonia; it is also a Roman colony. We spent several days there. On the Sabbath we went out of the city to the river–side, where we thought there would be a place where Jews gathered for prayer. We sat down and talked to the women who gathered there. One of those who heard us was Lydia from Thyatira, who was a dealer in purple cloth. She was a woman who worshipped God, and the Lord opened her mind to pay attention to what Paul was saying. After she and the people of her house had been baptized, she invited us:

Lydia   *Come and stay in my house if you have decided that I am a true believer in the Lord.*

Luke   *And she persuaded us to go.*

One day as we were going to the place of prayer, we were met by a slave–girl who had an evil spirit that enabled her to predict the future. She earned a lot of money for her owners by telling fortunes. She followed Paul and us, shouting:

Slave–girl   *These men are servants of the Most High God! They announce to you how you can be saved!*

Luke   *She did this for many days, until Paul became so upset that he turned round and said to the spirit:*

Paul   *In the name of Jesus Christ I order you to come out of her!*

Luke   *The spirit went out of her that very moment.* (Pause)

When her owners realized that their chance of making money was gone, they seized Paul and Silas and dragged them to the authorities in the public square. They brought them before the Roman officials [and said]:

Owner	*These men are Jews, and they are causing trouble in our city. They are teaching customs that are against our law; we are Roman citizens, and we cannot accept these customs or practise them.*
Luke	*And the crowd joined in the attack against Paul and Silas. Then the officials tore the clothes off Paul and Silas and ordered them to be whipped. After a severe beating they were thrown into jail, and the jailer was ordered to lock them up tight. Upon receiving this order, the jailer threw them into the inner cell and fastened their feet between heavy blocks of wood.*
Narrator	*About midnight Paul and Silas were praying and singing hymns to God, and the other prisoners were listening to them. Suddenly there was a violent earthquake, which shook the prison to its foundations. At once all the doors were opened, and the chains fell off all the prisoners. The jailer woke up, and when he saw the prison doors open, he thought that the prisoners had escaped; so he pulled out his sword and was about to kill himself. But Paul shouted at the top of his voice:*

Paul (loudly) *Don't harm yourself! We are all here!*

Narrator	*The jailer called for a light, rushed in, and fell trembling at the feet of Paul and Silas. Then he led them out [and asked]:*
Jailer	*Sirs, what must I do to be saved?*
Paul	*Believe in the Lord Jesus, and you will be saved — you and your family.*
Narrator	*Then they preached the word of the Lord to him and to all the others in his house. At that very hour of the night the jailer took them and washed their wounds; and he and all his family were baptized at once. Then he took Paul and Silas up into his house and gave them some food to eat. He and his family were filled with joy, because they now believed in God.*

When it was daylight, the magistrates sent
their officers to the jailer with the order:

Officer   Release those men.

Narrator   The jailer told Paul:

Jailer   The magistrates have ordered that you and
               Silas be released. Now you can leave. Go in
               peace.

Narrator   But Paul said to the officers:

Paul   They beat us publicly without a trial, even
               though we are Roman citizens, and threw us
               into prison. And now do they want to get rid of
               us quietly? No! Let them come themselves and
               escort us out.

Narrator   The officers reported this to the magistrates,
               and when they heard that Paul and Silas were
               Roman citizens, they were alarmed. They came
               to appease them and escorted them from the
               prison, requesting them to leave the city. After
               Paul and Silas came out of the prison, they
               went to Lydia's house, where they met with the
               brothers and encouraged them. Then they left.

2 CORINTHIANS 8.1–5

*Next, brothers, we will tell you of the grace of God which has
been granted to the churches of Macedonia, and how,
throughout continual ordeals of hardship, their unfailing joy
and their intense poverty have overflowed in a wealth of generosity on their part. I can testify that it was of their own
accord that they made their gift, which was not merely as far
as their resources would allow, but well beyond their
resources, and they had kept imploring us most insistently
for the privilege of a share in the fellowship of service to
God's holy people — it was not something that we expected
of them, but it began by their offering themselves to the Lord
and to us at the prompting of the will of God.*

Philippi was a leading city of Macedonia, and we can see in the
story of Acts 16.11–40 the beginnings of the Macedonian Church.
The first convert to Christianity on the European mainland was a
woman, an Asian travelling saleswoman, the head of a one–parent

family, perhaps an ex–slave. Her house became the first church in Europe.

Philippi had only recently been given the status of a Roman colony. On arrival there, the Christian movement came into the Roman and Latin world as never before. It also came into head–on conflict with paganism, not the gentle unsophisticated paganism of Lystra (Acts 14.8–18), but the cynical business of religion which could manipulate a girl's visions and exploit her commercially. The gospel was preached in answer to questions which were provoked by the apostles' challenge to religious and economic interests.

And so we come to the first European man to be baptized, a prison officer who had held a steady job in the colonial civil service, but whose life was shaken to its foundations by his encounter with the Christian mission.

So the Christian movement in Europe started in Macedonia, dramatically, and with controversy. The Church there, in the whole province and especially in Philippi and Thessalonica, was specially precious to Paul, and it was generous to him, both in financial support and supplying colleagues (Philippians 4.14–18; Acts 19.29). It continued to be a Church with significant female leadership (Philippians 4.2–3; Acts 17.4,12). Macedonia had been an area of conflict and opposition (1 Thessalonians 2.2), but it was also a place where Paul had been able to give completely of himself, and this appealed to their courage and generosity, so that the Macedonian Church became a suffering church, sharing in solidarity with the churches in Judaea (1 Thessalonians 2.7–16).

Macedonia was not a particularly privileged, wealthy, or cultured area compared to the sophisticated cities further south. Its gold mines had become exhausted, and the Roman colonial system soaked up the wealth produced by the extraction of other minerals, the salt trade, and the timber industry.

So Macedonia itself was a fairly poor area, the Christian movement there would have little in terms of wealth or status. The movement was new, had no government authorization, and had run into trouble from the start. So Paul speaks of the Macedonians' "poverty from the depths" (2 Corinthians 8.2).

In 2 Corinthians 8 and 9, Paul is first of all describing how the Macedonian Christians have sent help to the poor Christians in Jerusalem. Jerusalem was, of course, the starting–point of the Christian movement. It had become the poorest group of all. From the start, it had been based in the group of people called together by Jesus, and they had, on the whole, all come from the provincial peasant or artisan class. Then the Christian group had got into trouble with the local authorities, and the more mobile members had been scattered to places like Antioch (Acts 8.1). Even the leaders who gathered in Jerusalem for the epoch–making Council (Acts 15) were, socially and financially, unimportant people.

We can note a few details from Paul's account of the Macedonian Churches' generosity.

---

1. The Macedonians themselves asked to be allowed to share in the work of helping.

2. Three things made this possible: their experience of affliction (or trouble, or persecution), their joy, and their poverty. These three ingredients, added together, made a kind of fluid which lifted up their small wealth like a deposit of oil, and made it float and overflow.

3. What they gave was not their money but themselves. In fact, although this whole section is about money, the actual word money is never used.

With this background in mind, let the group think its way into the experience and the character of the Macedonian Church. It asks itself this set of questions:

Why do we, as the Church in Macedonia, find ourselves sending money to Christians in Jerusalem whom we've never met, and who are so different from us?

What is our motive and inspiration?

What has made it easy and what has made it difficult? Why do we respond as we do?

Perhaps the group might like to divide into two teams, one to look at the situation from the point of view of Lydia and her family and friends, and the other to look at it from the point of view of the prison officer and his family. Then the two teams should come together and share their ideas.

You will find it useful to write down a list of the main answers to this set of questions. This ought to help, when you consider questions concerning our own responses today.

Paul's argument could be expressed like this:

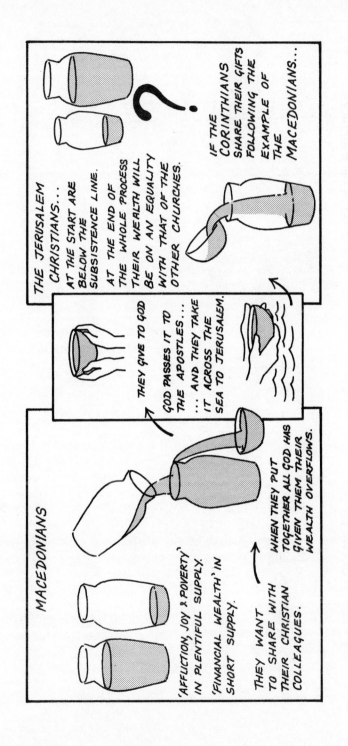

THE CHURCH OF MACEDONIA

They have a lot of wealth in the form of affliction, joy, and poverty.

They have little wealth in the form of money.

They put together their two kinds of wealth. The affliction, joy, and poverty lift the financial wealth and cause an overflow, which they give to God.

God gives it to the apostles to take to Jerusalem.

THE CHURCH OF JERUSALEM

They are very poor, below the subsistence line.

The gift from Macedonia brings them nearer to equality.

They will come to proper equality if the Church in Corinth behaves like the Church in Macedonia.

PRACTICAL PLANNING

1. How far do we see the Macedonians' reasoning and motives at work in ourselves?

2. Affliction and poverty aren't necessarily obstacles to generosity. People give what they can and God has his own way of doing the accounts (Mark 12.41–44). The Macedonians were very poor, but they begged for the favour of being allowed to contribute (2 Corinthians 8.4). Do you find this sort of thing in your church? Or in yourself? It is what we should expect, from the teaching of Jesus (e.g. Mark 10.23–30). And the experience of Third World Churches today confirms this. Watch out for stories from Christian Aid and other mission agencies to support this statement.

3. The Macedonians gave: first they gave themselves to God, as Paul had given himself to them (1 Thessalonians 2); then they gave to the apostles (2 Corinthians 8. 5). This is the right way round. When we give ourselves wholly to God, when we recognize his claim upon all our life and all our world, then our responsibility for money will fit into place. But sometimes we pay our money instead of giving ourselves. Can spiritual blessing flow from this? Should the Church accept money from people who do not worship?

4. The main purpose throughout these chapters (2 Corinthians 8 and 9) is that the giving of money should express and promote fellowship. Paul is very conscious that his churches are poor, but he doesn't talk of poverty as a problem, and he doesn't suggest that money can solve problems. Money is not a substitute for love but should be one expression of love. Our whole way of organizing society today implies that we think that money in itself has the power to cure all ills. Do you see ways in which the Church can help us to face this error?

UNIT 11 THE CHALLENGE TO THE CORINTHIANS

GETTING STARTED

- What sort of people are we in this group? See which members of the group feel that they fit into one or other of the following categories.

A. Are there some of you who have been in the Christian fellowship for a long time, who have always accepted Christian standards, and traditions, including charitable giving?

B. Are there some of you who were at one time more or less outside the Christian fellowship and then experienced some change which brought you in?

C. Are there some of you who don't have much education or social standing, but who belong to the church because it treats you seriously and makes you feel that you are a genuine member?

Let the members of the group form into three teams — each member should choose the team which he or she thinks fits them best.

Those members who are ministers, or leaders of some kind, should form a fourth team, D.

For a couple of minutes, the members meet in their teams so that they can briefly share their reasons for being there, and consider in what ways their experience makes them different to the other teams. (Don't be too rigid about which team to belong to: later in the session, we shall need these teams to be roughly equal in size, so try to get them evenly balanced at this stage.)

DIGGING DEEPER

If we look at the Acts of the Apostles and the letters of Paul, we find a lot of information about the Church in the city of Corinth.

There were evidently various types of people in that church, and they seem to have found it pretty difficult to get on with each other. We take three main types, and we may find that, in some ways, they are rather like some of the types of people in our church today.

Each team is to look at one of the types of people in the Church of Corinth.

Team A. APOLLOS' PARTY

You may find that you have something in common with Apollos. Apollos was a learned and respectable religious Jew from the great expatriate Jewish centre of learning at Alexandria (Acts 18.24–19.1), and a valuable person for this stage of the development of the Church (1 Corinthians 3.6). He was friendly with a local Jewish leader, Crispus, a synagogue–leader who had been willing to transfer to a house church next door to the synagogue when Christians were evicted (Acts 18.6–8). Apollos' party thought and felt as Jews, valued the Jewish traditions as their basic national identity — particularly in such a highly cosmopolitan city. But the Christian message had appealed to them, and they had taken the costly step of becoming Christian. Jesus for them was the fulfilment of the law of Moses. Jesus would make sense to them because of his spirit of generosity, compassion, and justice — qualities in which the law of Moses itself reflected the nature of God. Apollos and his friends would feel loyalty and sympathy and concern for their compatriots in Jerusalem.

Team B. GAIUS' GROUP

Another group of respectable persons, but Gentile converts. Some were people like Gaius himself, property owners and responsible citizens — Erastus, the City Treasurer or Director of Public Works, and Titius Justus, owner of substantial property, who had been a Gentile associate of the Jewish synagogue (1 Corinthians 1.14; Romans 16.23; Acts 18.7). For people in this group, Jewish identity and Jewish tradition in themselves would have no appeal. But the Jewish ideals of honesty, purity, and intellectual integrity were attractive and the new international citizenship of the Christian movement would make good sense (Galatians 3.28). At the same time, they (or some of them) would want to stand for the good name of their city. The group also included literate slaves, like Tertius, Paul's secretary in the Corinthian management, and others working in banking and the docks. Some of the wealthy members of this group might be the sort of people who, in the great city, made both a trade and a kind of game of lawsuits (1 Corinthians 6.1–8).

Team C. CHLOE'S CROWD

Probably the largest group, this was a bunch of recent converts from paganism — male and female slaves from the posh house-

holds, the markets, and the docks, from dozens of national back-
grounds and languages, with very little formal education, non-
citizens, pushed around by forces of employment, and by the
effects of the colonial system, who gravitated into the big city.
They complained about the insensitive behaviour of church members who were wealthier and had more control of their time: they
were last to arrive at gatherings — "never there on time" because
of their hours of work, so they sometimes found that there was no
supper left for them (1 Corinthians 11.20–21). Intellectual arguments would make little sense to them — even if they could
understand the languages of the learned; ecstasy, song, and dance
would make more sense (1 Corinthians 14). But they valued
Christian meetings because there they had the unique experience
of being treated as real people, with a voice and responsibility of
their own (1 Corinthians 12.13). More than the other groups, they
had everything to gain from a practical unity with other Christians,
so that they were the first to complain about divisions or cliques (1
Corinthians 1.11). Jesus was a poor man on the side of the poor,
and for them this would be part of the attraction of the Christian
movement as a sign of the nature of God. Most of them, as slaves,
would have little — if any — money to call their own.

Each of the teams A, B, and C should check through the information given above, looking up the biblical references given.

Ask yourselves questions like:

• What do we feel about this Corinthian Church of ours?

• What appeals to us?

• Why are we in it?

• What is difficult about it?

• What do we think of the other groups?

Team D is to take the part of Titus, Paul's messenger, who was
sent from Macedonia with two unnamed colleagues to convey the
letter which we are studying (2 Corinthians), and to try to get
Paul's plan implemented. He came as a kind of "stewardship
adviser". He knew the Church well; he was trusted by the members, but would realize what a mixed–up and irresponsible lot they
were. Paul could evidently rely on him (see 2 Corinthians 2.13;
7.6; 8.23; 12.17–18).

This team should first check through the information for teams A, B, and C above, so that it has some idea of the character of the Corinthian Church. Then it can start to look at the message about financial responsibilities which Titus has to deliver. (Chapters 8 and 9 of 2 Corinthians), and ask, "How do we think the Corinthian Church is going to respond?"

After about ten minutes, the Titus team should call for silence. A representative of the Titus team should address the "Church in Corinth" (teams A, B, and C). Titus should start by reminding them of Paul's message (1 Corinthians 16.1–4), acknowledging that this arrangement had not yet worked. Then Titus should read aloud to the other teams the whole of 2 Corinthians 8 and 9. While this is being read, the members of teams A, B, and C should, individually, mark in the margins of their books their responses to the message, staying within their characters of Apollos, Gaius, and Chloe. They should use the following symbols:

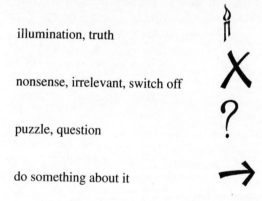

illumination, truth

nonsense, irrelevant, switch off

puzzle, question

do something about it

When the reading is over, teams A, B, and C meet separately again, to work out their understanding and their responses to what they have heard. Team D returns to the question of how they think the Church is going to respond.

After another ten minutes, Titus asks teams A, B, and C to face the straight question: "Are you going to take a collection to send to the Jerusalem Church or not?"

Allow five minutes or less for teams to discuss this. Then Titus says: "In order that we can get a proper decision about this, your different groups will have to consult each other. Apollos will send a delegate to Gaius, Gaius to Chloe and Chloe to Apollos, to see whether the three sections of the community agree." The delegates move as above, and the Titus team divides up to join the other teams, to listen to the debate, to advise if necessary, and to prepare to report back. The teams must stay within their characters for this phase.

After about ten minutes, Titus instructs the delegates to go back to their home teams: the Titus team reassembles, and the members share their experience for two or three minutes. Then Titus conducts the final process of making a decision: "Do you or don't you, as the whole Church in Corinth, agree to Paul's request?"

If you have a large group of people, you might like to form a fifth team, to work at the whole situation from the point of view of the Church in Jerusalem. This Church is a loyal, poor, fragile community of people who will easily feel left behind, and who are the starting–point of the whole movement. Let them suppose that a copy of Paul's letter has come into their hands. How will they feel about being on the receiving end of Paul's scheme? They accepted help from Antioch: but will they accept help from such a dodgy and undisciplined community as Corinth? Corinth (teams A, B, and C) could send a delegation to Jerusalem to discuss this.

Whatever the outcome of this debate, Titus should make sure that the reasons and motives for the decision are recognized. He needs to make sure that at least these two motives are recognized:

1. Giving is a sign of the gospel: it is the effect of the spirit of Jesus on human behaviour (2 Corinthians 8.9; 9.12–15). This is a motive in favour of Paul's request.
2. On the other hand, the Jerusalem Christians are far away, for most of us they are foreigners, and many of us will be as poor as they are. This would be a motive against Paul's request.

Which motive was eventually decisive?

PRACTICAL PLANNING

Come back into the present, the here and now. But recall the motives which led to the Corinthian Church's decision, according to your discussions. Do these motives have any effect as you handle your local church's budget and accounts?

• How far does your planning about money reflect the priorities of the gospel?

(Note: whatever the outcome of your debate, you can discover what the church in Corinth actually did decide by looking up Romans 15.26–27 — Corinth is situated in the province of Achaia.)

UNIT 12   CONTINUING WITH CORINTH

DIGGING DEEPER

You are, again, the Church in Corinth.

You have received Paul's letter, and the instructions concerning the collection of money. Now you have a new task. You are a group from the Church in Corinth which is being sent to another Church in the Province of Achaia to pass on the same teaching and message. (This fits in with what Paul says in Romans 15:26–27: Corinth was not the only Church in that Province to send money to Jerusalem.) Also, it doesn't matter overmuch what your decision was about the question in the last unit: the fact is that Corinth did indeed share in the giving to Jerusalem, although probably not all the members could have been totally involved.

There are three sides to the message — just as there are usually three sides to any Christian teaching — and if any of these sides is missing, the message will be incomplete and ineffective.

First, there is the message itself, based in the story of Jesus. Second, there is the meaning of the message for the Church as an organization and, through the Church, for the organization of the life of the world around. Third, there is the meaning of the message for the individual believer.

If the message is directed only at the organization, it will be hard for individuals to feel personal responsibility. And if the whole exercise is not based in the story of Jesus, it will become merely an exercise in competent administration, and the real sustaining motive will be missing. So the three sides belong together. Paul keeps them in mind all the time — thoroughly mixed-up, like the strands of a rope. But, like the strands of a rope, they can be distinguished.

So let the group divide into three teams. These should be new teams. Ideally, each team should contain at least one member from each of the teams from the previous unit.

Team A should read again through 2 Corinthians 8 and 9 and pick out the points where Paul is teaching about *the motive and purpose of Christian giving.*

Team B should read again through 2 Corinthians 8 and 9 and pick out the points where Paul is teaching about proper working of *the Church as an organization.*

Team C should read again through 2 Corinthians 8 and 9 and pick out the points where Paul is teaching about *the individual Christian's discipleship in practice.*

Each team should do this now, and make its own list of items, before attending to the points noted below.

Each team is to pick out the items which it would wish to put across as it goes to pass on Paul's message to another Church. You will need to feel that Paul's argument, at each point, is one which you can represent and interpret. How far do you find him convincing and helpful?

After making your own lists, consider the following points:

For Team A: The motive and purpose of Christian giving

1. In the middle of a quite practical discussion, Paul suddenly brings in the figure of Jesus (2 Corinthians 8.9). What exactly do you think Paul is trying to do here? An emotional arm–twisting? Presenting Jesus as a moral example? Or what? It's a strangely disconnected remark. If it were taken out, verse 8 would flow on quite naturally to verse 10. I suggest it's simply a reminder that the good news of Jesus Christ is that the heart of the universe is based on sharing: sharing is the very nature of God and we, in our little way, are caught up in that sharing. Question to the poorer members of the Church in Corinth — Chloe and the illiterate slaves: What does Jesus mean for you? In what ways do you feel you are becoming rich (or is this only after your death)? Question to the richer members: Are you becoming poor, like Jesus, like Chloe and her friends? Or, in some new way, are you becoming rich?

2. By making the collection, Paul was not appealing for some sort of project in Jerusalem: he was not asking for Corinthians to build a church there or employ a development worker. To do so would have meant that the Corinthians would have, in a sense, kept control of their money and used it to fulfil their own idea of what Jerusalem needed. It would have been giving with strings. Paul's purpose is quite simply to balance the buying–power of the two churches (2 Corinthians 8.13–15). Can you accept and persuade other people on these lines?

3. Equality is an end in itself, a proper aim, but inequality is a fact of life. There may have been all sorts of reasons why Jerusalem was poorer than Corinth, but Paul does not base his argument on these. He does not appeal for sympathy, nor does he dwell on the fact that the Jerusalem Christians were suffering for their faith. It seems that, for Paul, members of the Church simply ought to hold their wealth in common, and this principle was not overruled by the mere fact that the members might be 1,000 miles apart. This is voluntary justice. The fact that a group of

people lives according to this principle is itself good news. The Church fellowship is a movement for correcting the inequality in distribution of wealth which is the normal reality. This is sufficient motive for the collection. At some time in the future, the flow of wealth may move in the opposite direction (2 Corinthians 8.13–14). Does this convince you? Can you see yourselves trying to convince another church of this? (You will notice that, in a totally different situation, the basic ideals expressed in the law of Moses are being given new life here. The same God inspires the vision that wealth is to be shared, not accumulated.)

4. Nowhere does Paul try to argue that "Giving is Good for you". It isn't a kind of religious version of slimming! It isn't a matter of achieving success for yourself or making yourself feel good. It does create thanksgiving — not thanksgiving to the individual giver but thanksgiving to God: it will be God's gift and God's achievement: it will strengthen the bonds of fellowship, prayer, and rejoicing across the distances that separate churches from each other. This is the reward (2 Corinthians 9.8–15). Again, do you see yourselves putting this argument across to other people convincingly?

5. The purpose of all this appeal is to help the church members to give, to send money away. This is very different to church maintenance. Church maintenance is a matter of paying for what we receive. If we don't pay for the ministry and upkeep of our church, either someone else has to, or else it will have to close down. Paul points out this responsibility very simply in Galatians 6.6. But paying for services rendered is a quite different thing to real giving. Your Church in Corinth has a very wide range of people, from the richest to the poorest. Are you going to be able to show to others that you have been genuinely giving and not just paying?

For Team B: The Church as an organization

1. Notice the way in which Paul handles various methods of communication. At an earlier stage in its organization, the Church realized that for effective communication it needed both a clear written statement and a personal representative (Acts 15.22–32). Without the statement in writing, the messenger may not have sufficient authority: without the personal representative, the message will seem to be merely part of a bureaucratic system and will appeal only to the literate. Any plan for

effective communication has to include both. The written text, on its own, may communicate authority, but it is not likely to communicate faith. (Jesus left no written texts: we have the written texts of those who were given faith by their personal contact with him.) So, on this occasion Paul depends on his writing skill and on the personal word of Titus. As the Church in Corinth, you have been on the receiving end of this policy. How do you propose to apply it? Would you simply use Paul's text, or would you want to rewrite it?

2. How will you know whether the church which you are going to help is ready for you? You will realize (from comparing 1 Corinthians 16.1–4 with 2 Corinthians 8.10) that Paul had to make two attempts to get your programme at Corinth going. On the first occasion he gave you a very bare outline of the teaching. You seem to have got stuck, after making a good start, and he had to come back at you with a much more thorough teaching (in 2 Corinthians 8 and 9). Perhaps he remembered that the famine–relief appeal at Antioch had been successful because it had followed a year of systematic instruction (Acts 11.26–29). How will you ensure that your programme does not fizzle out?

3. How important do you think the money collection is? Do you, as a church, find it helpful to have such attention given to it? Does it embarrass you, or discourage you?

4. Paul was not reluctant to deal with the nuts and bolts of church finance himself, but he did try to keep it distinct from his pastoral work (1 Corinthians 16.2). He did not want to have collections going on during his apostolic visits (2 Corinthians 9.5). Do you agree with this?

5. Paul took good care over his public accountability in handling funds. The donor churches appointed their own representatives to ensure that the money was safely delivered: their task was to protect the money in transit, but not to try to dictate how it should be spent (2 Corinthians 8.16–24). Suppose the church which you are trying to help says, "We would be willing to give money to the Church in Jerusalem, but we want to make sure that they will spend it wisely." What will you answer?

For Team C: The individual Christian's discipleship in practice
1. The giving must be done by people who really feel free to give cheerfully and not under compulsion or threat (2 Corinthians 9.7). The Church itself can do a lot to provide a helpful atmosphere, not an atmosphere of anxiety and stress. Paul seems to

be specially keen to avoid a gloomy and anxious kind of caring (Romans 12.8). Do you think he succeeds, as far as your Church in Corinth is concerned?

2. The standard of giving is "each according to his or her means". There is no public fixed rate; it isn't a tax. Nor is it a proportion of our spending, like VAT. It must be voluntary. Church membership is not a commodity which costs the same for everyone (1 Corinthians 16.2; 2 Corinthians 8.12). So those who make the biggest financial contributions should not necessarily have the greatest authority in the Church. As you have looked at your experience of the Church in Corinth, do you feel that Paul has got this point across convincingly? Do the poor, the elderly, and the slaves really feel that they have the same status as the employers, the well–educated? Have you managed to handle the financial matters in such a way as to avoid some being first–class and some being second–class members?

3. What advice are you going to give to a fellow–Christian who wants help in working out his or her rate of contribution?

4. The Macedonians gave, voluntarily and spontaneously. But Paul urges his readers to plan ahead, to put the money on one side when they receive it, to work out their contribution responsibly (1 Corinthians 16.2; 2 Corinthians 9.7). Our contribution should not be suddenly decided on the spur of the moment. Paul shows that it's possible both to plan intelligently and to give cheerfully. In your experience of trying out Paul's advice, do you think that it works? Will you commend it to others?

5. Christian giving is a duty, certainly, but above all, it is a grace given by God (2 Corinthians 8.1,7; 9.14). Just as we are supposed to increase in other forms of grace, such as love and faith, so we should expect to grow in the grace of cheerful giving. Can you go to another church and testify, from your experience in Corinth, that it does work like this?

PLEASE NOTE
1. Don't rush this stage. If you feel that you need two full meetings for each team, never mind. These two chapters of 2 Corinthians are very packed and, when you look at it closely, you may find Paul's teaching quite hard to accept.

2. Do stay within the "Church in Corinth" situation, and don't get side–tracked into your present–day situation. There will be plenty of opportunity for that. The idea, of the present exercise is that it's worthwhile to use our imagination to feel what Paul's

message would have meant to those for whom it was first written. The Church in Corinth had enormous problems. As we have seen, it had quite a extraordinary range of types of people in its membership. It's no accident that Paul's great "hymn of love" (1 Corinthians 13) is addressed to the Church in Corinth: only the supernatural love of God could possibly hold such a collection of misfits in one body. If an appeal like this in 2 Corinthians 8 and 9 could make practical sense in Corinth, it could work anywhere.

At the end of this unit, each team will have its own list of points of interest, plus its own comments on the five concerns suggested for each team above. The teams should briefly get together to share their statements with each other, preferably written up on large sheets of paper which can be kept for reference next time.

PRACTICAL PLANNING

We stay with 2 Corinthians 8 and 9, but we come into our own here–and–now. This will probably take at least one complete session and could well spread over a longer time. Again, it is important not to rush this stage, because this is the point at which the Bible study should have its effect in public and personal policy.

Take the fifteen questions given to the teams in the previous "Digging Deeper" unit starting on page 78. You may find it simplest to stay with the three teams: or you might find some other way of handling this phase. Take those questions, and try to answer them in relation to your own local church community. Compare these answers with the answers given when you were imagining yourselves to be the Church in Corinth. You may find that the following questions help to develop your discussion.

Team A

A1. Paul clearly believed that the poverty of Jesus is part of his saving character. Jesus shared the status and the limitations of the poor of his day.

• How far, in your church, do you have the sense that Jesus is particularly close to the poor, and that the poor have some particular kind of authority? Or, in your church, are those in leadership positions the same sort of people who have leadership positions in the world around?

A2. On the whole, missionary societies and development agencies find that British Christians are more willing to give to projects controlled from Britain than to give money for our overseas partners to spend as they see fit.

- Why is this?

- What do we do about it?

A3. There are many different reasons why people donate money to agencies helping the poor.

- Is the main reason for giving a need to satisfy our conscience, or to overcome the inequalities which cause poverty?

- Do you feel that the correction of inequality is a sufficient motive, as it was for Paul? Would you push this further, and say that our problem today is not to make the rich give to the poor but to stop the rich taking from the poor?

- Can you separate issues associated with unequal distribution of wealth from such problems as international debt and trading systems which operate to the disadvantage of primary producers?

A4. How conscious is your church of its membership of an international fellowship of sharing? As well as giving, as well as praying, are you also giving thanks? Are you continually praising God for the international Church as a sign of his purpose of making peace?

A5. It is important to recognize the distinction between paying and giving.

- How far do you clarify in your own church's finances the distinction between paying and giving?

- Do you know how much it actually costs for you to receive the various ministries and services which you receive from the Church?

- Of the money which you contribute weekly, what proportion do you intend to be used as payment for what you receive i.e. for maintenance of your local church life, ministers, buildings etc., and what proportion do you intend to be given away? Have you told your treasurer of your intentions?

- Would you welcome a church finance system which gave you more opportunity to make this sort of distinction?

Team B

B1. Paul took great care to combine effectively his use of written material and personal communication.

- How well is your local church handling this task?

B2. It seems that timing is important in the strategy for stewardship. Without proper teaching in advance, a financial project can be disappointing, and can do more harm than good. But the wrong sort of delay can be mere faithlessness, and can mean that good work does not get done.

- Are you getting the balance right?

- How do you approach the education of children and young people? Can a person ever be too young to be taught about this sort of responsibility?

B3. Paul treated the offering of money as something very important, rich in meaning and representing great commitment. In many churches we do not treat the worshipper's money offering as a significant part of the worship.

- Can you really mean your offering if you are expected to make it at the same time as you are singing a hymn?

- Can you suggest improvements in the way in which we handle this part of our liturgy?

B4. Paul did try to keep financial matters distinct from pastoral work (1 Corinthians 16. 2; 2 Corinthians 9. 5).

- Do you feel that this is a useful distinction for your local church?

- How far do you think your ministers should be involved in financial management and leadership?

  (This is a matter on which there is not an ideal answer: there are dangers in both directions. But it is a matter on which both ministers and lay leaders need to know each other's minds: otherwise there is an open field for misunderstanding and for incorrect assumptions.)

B5. Paul took good care over his accountability — he arranged for proper handling of all cash and assets.

- How satisfactory is your church's accountability? How far do your members know how money is handled?

- Are the accounts presented so that people who are not financial specialists can feel that they can themselves answer for the church's financial workings and take some responsibility for them?

Team C

C1. Money often seems to be a gloomy and burdensome issue, for individuals and for churches — especially for churches! There may be all sorts of special reasons for anxiety, such as inherited buildings, but the underlying attitude ought to be of cheerfulness (2 Corinthians 9.7; Romans 12.8).

- Are you and your church cheerful about money?

- On the whole, the witness of biblical writers is that you don't have to be rich to be cheerful — the more money you have the more anxious you are likely to be. This is remarkably difficult for churches in our part of the world to believe. Do you believe it?

C2. Some ways of thinking and of planning for church finance do have the effect of making two tiers of membership, those who can pay a lot and who can fully and publicly join in elaborate schemes, and those who can't. More than any other single thing, it is this danger which has made many of us very hesitant about stewardship programmes.

- Do you feel that you take this into account in your local church? Can you suggest ways of improvement? Have you yourself worked through your worries about this sort of problem?

- Paul says that the poorer Macedonians begged to be allowed to contribute to the collection (2 Corinthians 8.4). Do you and your church really encourage sincerely the weakest, youngest, and the poorest to contribute? Or do you feel, deep down, that they should be let off?

C3. Church contributions are not like income tax or VAT or any other fixed rate.

- How do you work out an appropriate level of contribution for yourself?

C4. The modern word for what Paul is saying in 1 Corinthians 16.2 and 2 Corinthians 9.7 is "budgeting". There is a place for spontaneous generosity but we need to be reliable. Those who receive our contribution need to be able to depend upon it, and that will not be possible if we always leave it to the feelings of the moment.

- Does your church encourage reliable budgeting?

  Most churches produce income and expenditure accounts, but these are essentially backward–looking. Not all local churches produce budgets: but where they do, they show that they have thought out their plans ahead. They consider what can be tackled and what will have to be left aside, and this will encourage individual members to take their part more responsibly.

- Do you take an active interest in your local church's budgeting?

C5. If Christian giving is, indeed, a grace given by God, do you see yourself growing in it? Are you better at it than you used to be — not just in money but in your total giving of yourself, your recognition that everything you have is on loan from the true owner?

Even in the case of those of us who are not good at it, our ability to give is still a grace given by God, not a desperate struggle for self–improvement. Paul uses all sorts of arguments to encourage us to be generous, but he carefully steers clear of manipulating us by guilt. He doesn't blame or scold. It is the person who is free from a sense of guilt who will be most able to make a genuine gift, a gift which is itself not designed to make anyone else feel guilty or inferior or second–class.

At the end of your working in teams, the teams come together and share their findings with each other. If you made written statements as suggested at the end of the previous unit, bring these out and compare those statements with the statements arising from your work in teams for this unit.

Then, decide what to do with the ideas and judgements which you have shared. There may well be matters which you will wish to send on to the leaders of your church, or new commitments which you want to make about your own discipleship.

SECTION E
BACK TO BASICS

UNIT 13 THE PURPOSE OF IT ALL

GETTING STARTED

Bring a few ordinary, manufactured things to the meeting — a boot, a fork, a teapot, or perhaps something like a tennis racket, or a flute. Try your best to describe the thing just according to the way it is made, the material, the appearance, the shape, without any reference to the purpose for which it is made. How long can you talk about it without bringing in the purpose?

DIGGING DEEPER

Before ending this course on stewardship, we need to get back to the purpose of the whole enterprise. Stewardship is the proper management of resources on behalf of the owner. The purpose in the mind of the owner is essential. Sometimes it seems that we think that the Church is all right if we have got the correct management system, or if the maintenance arrangements are going smoothly. The boss of a supermarket or a football club would not be so easily satisfied: they would look for achievement of the purpose for which the enterprise exists — the production of profits or the attainment of goals.

So, what do you see as the purpose of the Church?

---

1. What do you, as an individual, want the Church for? What purpose does it serve for you personally?

2. What does the Church seem to think that its purpose is, in its public policy or activities?

The group can break up into little teams to consider these questions, and then reconvene to put their answers together.

Now read Mark 3.13–19 (from *The Dramatised Bible*).

Narrator	*Jesus went up a hill and called to himself the men he wanted. They came to him, and he chose twelve, whom he named apostles. [He told them:]*
Jesus	*I have chosen you to be with me. I will also send you out to preach, and you will have authority to drive out demons.*
Narrator	*These are the twelve he chose: Simon –*
Commentator	*Jesus gave him the name Peter.*
Narrator	*James and his brother John –*
Commentator	*The sons of Zebedee. Jesus gave them the name Boanerges, which means "Men of thunder".*
Narrator	*Andrew, Philip, Bartholomew, Matthew, Thomas, James –*
Commentator	*The son of Alphaeus.*
Narrator	*Thaddaeus, Simon –*
Commentator	*The Patriot.*
Narrator	*And Judas Iscariot –*
Commentator	*Who betrayed Jesus.*

Here we have a statement of Jesus' purpose in calling his disciples, in forming his team of workers. It is a short basic statement containing three objectives which can provide headlines for our work.

1. Jesus called people to be with him. That is a purpose in itself. They were to share his company, to observe him, to absorb his ideas, attitudes, habits, to learn by being alongside him. They were to be a team together. They had no special previous qualifications. Later on, they would still, for the most part, be obviously uneducated in the usual sense of the word but they would be recognizable as graduates of his school — they had been with Jesus (Acts 4.13).

   If we were wanting to make a good team, we would look for people who would be able to work well together, who would form a friendly community, who would be natural cooperators.

Jesus seems to have been determined to gather a collection of misfits — Matthew the collaborator with the Roman tax–system; Simon the Zealot, a member of a terrorist movement which was planning to get rid of the Romans by force; two ambitious and jumpy characters who got the name "Thunder's Kids"; a thoroughly unreliable person in the senior position. Altogether, a group of people who constantly got in the way and were a good deal less clear–sighted than the poor and blind whom their master sought to serve (e.g. Mark 8.14–21; 10.13–16; 10.35–52). Jesus was starting off a movement which would not depend upon people being able to get on with each other naturally, but would depend only on his call and power. The same quickly happened in the days of the Acts of the Apostles, when the Church grew by drawing in a wider and wider range of people.

So Jesus called disciples to make a new kind of fellowship.

2. Jesus called people to be sent out to preach, to communicate the good news that the kingdom of God is near, that there is a new opportunity for God's authority to work in the world, and that therefore it's worthwhile to make the necessary radical changes.

3. Jesus called people to be sent out to stand against the powers that caused people to be less complete than the creator intended. They were to go to challenge the powers of evil, to bring healing and peace as signs of the kingdom of God.

So there are three purposes for the formation of the team. The first is the maintenance of the fellowship of the team by being with Jesus, the other two purposes are tasks for the team to fulfil towards society around. The disciples learn their work by means of what we would call industrial placement or a sandwich course — a time of learning with the teacher, a time applying the teaching out in the field, then a return to the teacher (Luke 9 and 10).

All working groups need this balance. Unless there is a real task to be done, members will just lose interest, or spend their energy on internal squabbling. Unless there is a genuine fellowship of maintenance and mutual support, members will be valued only in terms of their success and not because of their value as persons. They will wear out themselves and each other, and there will be no room for the slower or less able or less qualified.

PRACTICAL PLANNING

Look at your own local church or group of churches. Look again at your own statements of what you see to be the purpose of the church. How do your purposes match the purposes for which Jesus calls disciples? Do you want the church for the same reasons that Jesus wants the church?

Traditionally, a Christian mission station has three elements — a church building, a school, and a hospital or clinic. These represent the three purposes of the disciple group:

---

1. To be with Jesus and with each other, "abiding" in the love of God, being nourished through word and sacrament, having the human will shaped and reshaped by contact with God in worship.

2. To educate, to communicate, to spread knowledge.

3. To attack the sources of disease, ill–health, poverty, and injustice, and to spread peace and cooperation.

   Go through the programme of your local church and see how far you are fulfilling these three purposes.

- Who is doing these things?
- How are they reported and shared?
- What is their place on the budget?

(Bear in mind that not all of God's work and interests come under the control of synods or church councils! Much that is done by followers of Jesus under item 3, for instance, may be done in secular structures, local authorities, the health service, voluntary organizations, political movements, and so on. But Christians still ought to feel that this is part of their discipleship, and that their Christian colleagues should take an intelligent and supporting interest in their efforts. How often does your local church hear about the problems and opportunities faced in your schools, medical practices, local radio, housing departments etc.?)

Is your church naturally friendly? Do members get on easily with each other? If they do, why is this? Is it because you love each other with God's supernatural love, or because you have managed to avoid having awkward people?

UNIT 14   THE DEATH AND LIFE OF THE STEWARD

GETTING STARTED

Have a look round and see what can be made out of "rub-bish" — the discarded stuff with no more life in it. Have you or your children made anything by recycling?

- What was the original use?

- What is its use now?

- How did you get the idea?

DIGGING DEEPER

Stewardship, we have seen all along, is about management. So, we try to be better managers. If we manage to do all our tasks for God better, perhaps we may fulfil the whole purpose and have a successful enterprise. It looks as if it might just be possible, with a bit more care and dedication.

And then we are hit by something in the gospel which goes beyond what is possible. Going with Jesus takes us beyond good management, beyond struggle, organization, and results. It has got something to do with going down with him to loss, to death, being with people who are surrounded by loss, sharing their death.

Your group could divide into two teams, to consider two different parts of the gospel story.

A: MARK 10.17–27
(From *The Dramatised Bible*)

Narrator   As Jesus was starting on his way again, a man ran up and knelt before him.

Man   Good Teacher, what must I do to receive eternal life?

[Narrator Jesus asked him:]

Jesus   Why do you call me good? No one is good except God alone. You know the commandments: "Do not commit murder; do not commit adultery; do *not steal; do not accuse anyone falsely; do not cheat; respect your father and your mother."*

Man   *Teacher, ever since I was young, I have obeyed all these commandments.*

Narrator   *Jesus looked straight at him with love.*

Jesus   *You need only one thing. Go and sell all you have and give the money to the poor, and you will have riches in heaven; then come and follow me.*

Narrator   *When the man heard this, gloom spread over his face, and he went away sad, because he was very rich.* (Pause)

                    Jesus looked round at his disciples:

Jesus   *How hard it will be for rich people to enter the Kingdom of God!*

Narrator   *The disciples were shocked at these words [but Jesus went on to say:]*

Jesus   *My children, how hard it is to enter the Kingdom of God! It is much harder for a rich person to enter the Kingdom of God than for a camel to go through the eye of a needle.*

Narrator   *At this the disciples were completely amazed [and asked one another:]*

Disciple
(aside)   *Who, then, can be saved?*

Narrator   *Jesus looked straight at them and answered:*

Jesus   *This is impossible for man, but not for God; everything is possible for God.*

MARK 8.34–35

Then he called the people to him, as well as his disciples, and said to them, "anyone who wants to be a follower of mine must renounce self: he must take up his cross and follow me. Whoever wants to save his life will lose it, but whoever loses his life for my sake and for the Gospel's will save it."

What Jesus requires of the rich man is a lot more than competent stewardship. It is financial suicide. It goes against most religious advice, ancient or modern — fulfil your potential, develop your self–expression, expand your self–awareness. Jesus invites the rich man to join himself to the poorest of the land, the companions of Jesus, who never had any space for a potential of their own, whose only means of self–expression would be dismissed as vandalism or terrorism, who were not allowed any real self to be aware of. "Deny yourself and take up your cross," would mean, quite simply, take your place among those whom the ruling authorities would consider dangerous and expendable. No one carried a cross except under compulsion. No one carried a cross except people who were reckoned to be dangerous to the security of the state. No one carried a cross except on the way to death.

Stewardship has to be conformed to the priorities of Jesus: otherwise it can be just another way of dodging our discipleship, by trying to get our self–fulfilment through a "successful" church. It's not impossible for a group of humble, generous Christian individuals to gang up to make a proud, aggressive and churlish church. The aim of self–fulfilment has been the pretext for every kind of cruelty of race against race, creed against creed, generation against generation. Self–fulfilment appeals to the idea of endless expansion, the motive for accumulating more and more wealth, and getting more and more experiences (including religious experiences). But the call to deny oneself and carry only a cross — that's totally impossible!

The secret is that when we are called and claimed by God we are totally affirmed, totally valued. Any way of claiming value for ourselves in competition with others, any way of affirming ourselves by wealth, achievement or race would be as much as to say that we do not need God's valuing of us. Paul summed it up once for all in the most personal and most universal of his statements:

"I have been crucified with Christ: it is no longer I who live, but Christ who lives in me, and the life I now live in the flesh I live by faith in the Son of God, who loved me and gave himself for me" (Galatians 2.20).

- From all this, is there one idea which seems to you to lead you forward?

B: JOHN 12.20–33
(From *The Dramatised Bible*)

Narrator	*Some Greeks were among those who had gone to Jerusalem to worship during the festival. They went to Philip — he was from Bethsaida in Galilee — and said:*
Greeks 1&2	*Sir –*
Greek 2	*We want to see Jesus.*
Narrator	*Philip went and told Andrew, and the two of them went and told Jesus. Jesus answered them:*
Jesus	*The hour has now come for the Son of Man to receive great glory. I am telling you the truth: a grain of wheat remains no more than a single grain unless it is dropped into the ground and dies. If it does die, then it produces many grains. Whoever loves his own life will lose it; whoever hates his own life in this world will keep it for life eternal. Whoever wants to serve me must follow me, so that my servant will be with me where I am. And my Father will honour anyone who serves me.*
	Now my heart is troubled — and what shall I say? Shall I say "Father, do not let this hour come upon me"? But that is why I came — so that I might go through this hour of suffering. Father, bring glory to your name!
Narrator	*Then a voice spoke from heaven:*
Voice	*I have brought glory to it, and I will do so again.*
Narrator	*The crowd standing there heard the voice, and some of them said it was thunder, while others said:*
Person 1	*An angel spoke to him!*
Narrator	*But Jesus said to them:*

| Jesus | *It was not for my sake that this voice spoke, but for yours. Now is the time for this world to be judged; now the ruler of this world will be overthrown. When I am lifted up from the earth, I will draw everyone to me.* |
| Narrator | *In saying this he indicated the kind of death he was going to suffer.* |

Jesus, at this point in John's Gospel, is at the height of his success. His opponents cannot stop his reputation growing: foreigners are becoming interested in him. Jesus realizes that there has to be a change of direction. His way forward is not to be by continuous expansion of fame and influence, but through death. If you have a grain of wheat, you can either make food out of it now, or you can dump it in the ground where it will die in producing a harvest. (The process is more obvious with potatoes — the seed potato ends up as a rotten mess among a new crop of potatoes.) Jesus sees that life and renewal for the world will come through a new kind of publicity, a publicity not of his power to heal but of his obedience to the point of death. This is not a gloomy mood of self–hatred or self–destruction. He knows that he is valued and precious: therefore he is free to be cast aside. The voice of the Father affirms him (compare Mark 9.7) so he is free to deny himself. He is loved, so he does not have to be preoccupied with preserving his own value. And the same will be true of those who follow and serve him.

But it isn't easy and obvious, he argues within himself; it doesn't all come automatically (this is where the image of the seed and the harvest breaks down). Resurrection is not an inevitable process. It needs a painful decision and he is in turmoil. The resurrection of Jesus was not just a working out of natural forces. The resurrection was a costly defeat of the destructive forces of sin and darkness which brought upon Jesus the particular kind of death which he suffered. In his resurrection is the defeat of all the injustice, carelessness about truth, fear, impatience, contempt for the weak, which lay behind the death not only of Jesus but of thousands of people destroyed in similar ways.

This is the most fully Christian statement about life: the new does not come through the survival of the old but through the death of the old. A Church that seeks to proclaim Christ's life needs first to follow Christ in death. What, in practice, can this mean?

> • From this study, is there one idea which seems to lead you forward?

Let the two teams come together and share their findings, their ideas for ways forward.

PRACTICAL PLANNING

You may find that no "practical plans", as such, come out of this study.

Perhaps you will feel that a question mark is placed against the whole idea of planning.

But you can ask this:

> What do you feel is the main motive of your church?
>
> • Maintenance?
>
> • Preservation?
>
>   or
>
> • Transformation?

Bear in mind that these two gospel passages come to us from a community of disciples which knew about resurrection. They told these stories because they could see that God's strange method works. The one who does deny himself and takes up his cross is declared by God to be Lord and Christ. The one who is treated as valueless, who shares the fate and experience of the most valueless people, is claimed by God as the one of supreme value (Acts 2.30). Our stewardship is a stewardship of that message, which turns most practical planning on its head.

You may well be able to see this sort of process at work, in the Church, in the world around, in your own life. There is this mystery of hope that keeps faith alive in the most unlikely places. Do you see death and resurrection happening? Do you see signs that God is, in some way, bringing life through death, affirmation through denial? Is there something going on in which God is beckoning you to cooperate?

Don't rush this! After all the management details about stewardship, this may lead to the "one thing needful" for your discipleship. So be willing to wait, to be silent, to listen doubly carefully to each other's hesitant vision or expectant pain. Be willing to take others into your darkness. Be willing to be taken by others into their darkness.

And the risen Christ will be there.

THE EARTH IS THE LORD'S
(Psalm 24)

JOHN BELL

ANTIPHON (may be sung in harmony)

The _ earth is the Lord's and _ all that is in it; the _ World and it's peo - ple be - long to the Lord.

VERSES (unison)

1. All that ex - ists, all _ crea - tures and kinds, all wo - men and men to their Ma - ker be - long; _ un - der the seas God _

© Wild Goose Publications

foun - ded the earth and plan - ted it firm in the depths of the

(to ANTIPHON)

waves.

† ♩ ♩ in v.5 only

* in v.2 only

v1 Cantor A   All that exists, all creatures and kinds,
                  all women and men to their Maker belong;
                  under the seas God founded the earth
                  and planted it firm in the depths of the waves.   *(Antiphon)*

v2 Cantor B   Who may go up to the mountain of God
                  and who may appear in the Lord's holy place?
    Cantor A   The one with clean hands, whose heart is kept pure,
                  who shuns what is false and forsakes all deceit.   *(Antiphon)*

v3 Cantor A   Those who receive the blessing of God
                  know that their salvation is found in the Lord.
    Cantor B   This is the witness of those who enquire
                  who long for the presence of Jacob's own God.   *(Antiphon)*

v4 Chorus   Fling wide the gates and open the doors
                  and so let the great King of Glory come in.
    Cantor A   Who is this king to enter these gates?
    Chorus   The Lord strong and mighty in battle is he.   *(Antiphon)*

v5 Chorus   Gates everlasting, now lift yourselves up
                  that the great King of Glory might enter within.
    Cantor A   Who is this great king that the gates should be raised?
    Chorus   The mighty and strong Lord of Hosts is his name.   *(Antiphon)*

The verses are best sung as indicated in order that the dialogical
nature of the psalm is experienced. Cantor A represents a priestly
figure who acts as the respondent to the questions of the community
of pilgrims (Cantor B and Chorus).